LIVING WITH A SPIRITUAL WARRIOR

Also by Jesus Garcia:

The Love of a Master
The Dreams of a Master

LIVING WITH A SPIRITUAL WARRIOR

A PRACTICAL TREATISE

By Rev. Jesus Garcia, D.S.S.
Scott J-R Publishing

© 2020
Scott J-R Productions. ® All rights reserved
ISBN 978-0-9996010-4-4
Library of Congress Control Number: 2020919746
Proofread by Nancy O'Leary
Cover Artwork by David Sand
Cover and Interior Design by Ana Arango

Submitted
in partial fulfillment of the requirements for
the Doctor of Spiritual Science Degree

From
Peace Theological Seminary and College of Philosophy
Los Angeles, California

November 2007
Draft 2 – January 2008
Draft 3 – May 2008

*This practical treatise
is dedicated
to
Dr. John-Roger,
my teacher,
my friend, my wayshower,
my Spiritual Warrior*

*Spiritual Warriors are people—men and women—
who confidently make choices
about where to focus their internal attention,
even when the external realities of
their everyday lives
are chaotic, troublesome,
or just plain annoying.*

– John-Roger
Spiritual Warrior:
The Art of Spiritual Living
(Source: www.lovingeachday.org)

Table of Contents

1. Introduction *1*
2. Heroes *9*
3. Finding My Outer Spiritual Warrior and J-R *17*
4. Finding My Inner Spiritual Warrior *33*
5. The Travels of a Mystical Traveler *39*
6. The Class *47*
7. D.S.S. Intentions *51*
8. Hypothesis *55*
9. Designing My Individual Study *59*
10. Outcomes *65*
11. Being Patient with Myself *87*
12. Ten-Week Repeatability Study with Others *93*
13. Conclusions *101*
14. Epilogue *105*
15. Appendix I–Ordination Blessing *109*
16. Appendix II–Glossary *115*
17. Appendix III–References & Bibliography *129*
18. About the Author *133*

*Spiritual Warriors have the Sword of their Heart
in front of them. They use awareness as
their primary weapon, and their armor is
their intention. If your intention is
to be loving and caring, that means
you cannot let anything that is not loving
or not caring come in.*

– JOHN-ROGER, D.S.S.

Introduction

ॐ

I chose for the title of my Practical Treatise (P.T.): "Living with a Spiritual Warrior." My life is full of people who have influenced and loved me in ways that I could not have imagined. These people, good or bad, were Spiritual Warriors. Being a Spiritual Warrior, to me, is pretty much taking the ups and downs of life and learning from it all.

I am a student in MSIA—the Movement of Spiritual Inner Awareness. Dr. John-Roger, D.S.S., founded the Movement of Spiritual Inner Awareness in 1968 as a vehicle for teaching Soul Transcendence (* Marks glossary entries—see glossary for definition). He has given over 5,000 Seminars and written over 50 books. His book, *You Can't Afford the Luxury of a Negative Thought*, became a *New York Times* #1 Best-Seller. As part of my personal studies, other books by John-Roger that molded me, and prepared me for writing this P.T. and for making the film *Spiritual Warriors*, were: *Passage Into Spirit*, *The Way Out Book*, *The Spiritual Promise*, *Loving Each Day*, *Fulfilling Your Spiritual Promise*, and many more. The J-R Videotapes along with *The Wayshower* tape packet was very insightful to me regarding how J-R became who he is today. MSIA has so many tools that assist me. But, above them all, my greatest learning has come through my direct physical and spiritual contact with John-Roger.

In 1999, after two years of study at Peace Theological Seminary and College of Philosophy towards the Master of Spiritual Science degree, I began the Doctor of Spiritual Science program (D.S.S.), a four-year course of study for which this Practical Treatise is required for graduation. In 1997, Dr. John-Roger had written the book *Spiritual Warrior: The Art of Spiritual Living*. The ideas he wrote about spoke to me and became important to me; they provided me with a framework to live my life. Being a Spiritual Warrior became my goal. Before I began the D.S.S. program, John-Roger and I had written a film script based upon his book that would change my life. It was called "Spiritual Warriors," which depicts the journey of a young man as he awakens to his spiritual awareness and potential gifts through reincarnation dreams. The beginning of production of the film paralleled my studies for my P.T. I began to see that the film was a tool for greater awakening, both as a student and in life.

Being a Spiritual Warrior, to me, is pretty much taking both the ups and downs of life and learning from them all. There are things in my life that really came at me to destroy me, and they could have either finished me off or I could spin them, make them funny, and let them roll off me like a rain drop. I could make them stepping-stones towards growing and bettering myself. I go through my sorrows and my tears, and as I write those things out, I express those experiences; I look on the bright side and I stay in the present. I move on and breathe, and I meditate. I'm grateful that I am an actor because, during the worst times of my life, I was able to express my feelings through a movie, a TV show, a play, and also through singing and writing songs. So, at those worst times of my life, and there have been a few, I was able to

Introduction

create gorgeous work, whether it be a song or a script or acting in a scene or a play. I could really get it all out for that moment. I created love.

When I was, maybe, eight or nine years old, I was in Orlando, Florida, at my auntie's house. She was a beautiful woman. I loved her. I felt so much love from her. I loved it when I would rest my head on her lap while she brushed my hair with her fingers. Back in the days when kids could hang out in the front seat with no seat belts, we would take long drives with my mother while I slept on Auntie's lap. She was my favorite relative, second to my grandmother, of course. For some reason, I was staying at her house. My mother and father were always doing something, so I was left at other people's houses, mainly my auntie's. I remember walking to school, maybe about a mile, or a mile and a half, and seeing a lot of spider webs along the roadside—big spiders. It's a very tropical climate in Orlando, Florida. And I remember in the afternoons eating oranges to quench my thirst from the blazing heat, playing with my train set in the cool evenings, and trying to make sense of my life, to no avail.

One night in my room, when I was in a twilight sleep, I remember seeing a man in a white suit, angelic looking. He was standing by the entrance to my room. It was nothing negative but very mysterious. The next day came; I never said anything to anyone, and that evening my auntie told her friends at dinner that she had seen a spirit. She didn't know who it was, so she thought it was the same person who had lived in the house before us, who had died in the house years ago; she could only assume that it was the ghost of that person. I believed my auntie because I had seen the Ghost-Spirit too. Later, when my mother came to take me home, she confessed to us that she saw the Spirit-Man too. I felt we were tapping into something spiritual. But I didn't understand what to do with this talent.

When I was growing up in Florida with my mother and my stepfather, I had access to learning about Mormons, Jehovah's Witnesses, and Christians. I'm just really thankful for all the different kinds of influences, the culturally diverse experiences I had growing up. I thank all of those people because of how much that just really opened my consciousness and my mind, so it's not about just one religion. It is one God and many roads.

I first came to Los Angeles around the time Bruce Lee died in 1973. That was my connection to L.A. when I first came. My mother and I moved in with my grandfather and his friends, and these two ladies let us stay at their place. Eventually, we moved across the street and got our own place, around Temple and Rampart. I later learned that in all of the places that John-Roger had ever been to, he was planting light columns for all of us to walk through in that neighborhood. I lived in many of the places he lived in Los Angeles, including on Las Palmas in Hollywood, where I used to play guitar, and on Coronado by Alvarado and Temple.

Every night I'd go to sleep listening to an AM radio. It was a really lonely time in my life, in a really weird place and time. I would sleep underneath the covers because I would see things and feel things very near to me. One of the things I kept seeing and feeling was this purple circle with no pattern that would pulsate from the right side of my mind, the very thing I had seen for the first time as a young boy. It wasn't until years later, when I first started in the Movement of Spiritual Inner Awareness and I was doing my S.E.'s,* that I saw it again and started to understand. It probably happens to a lot of people, where we experience something and it scares us, and we don't know what to do with it, so we hide it and forget that it ever happened to us. However, if we do some kind of studying that educates us, we lead ourselves into this sacred path, the Mystery School* of Spirit, and then say, "Hey, that makes perfect sense. That purple light is the Master of the

Introduction

inner realms, the Mystical Traveler,* the Master inside the Sound Current.*" And we awaken our consciousness, the Third Eye.*

Years later, in Los Angeles, I was invited to go to a teen seminar. I had heard that my favorite actor was going to be there, David Hubbard. His TV show, *James at 16*, was a mega-hit. I wanted to meet him because I wanted to be a star too. He was leading this event, which offered a safe place for teens to share their problems. Boy, I had a lot of problems, mainly hormones and girls. Little did I know that David represented one of John-Roger's organizations called Insight Seminars.* When I arrived at the event, there in the front entrance of the house I saw, on the mantel of the welcoming area, a picture of a man in a white suit, looking very angelic. He looked like the same man in Orlando, the Ghost-Spirit man that my auntie and I saw. I started to realize that I must know this man somehow; I just hadn't put it together yet. I saw the qualities that I wanted in that very moment, the essence of something great. Yet the specific details eluded me.

I've had a sense of the Spirit my whole life. When I was younger it seemed to me that as we grow older the veil drops and the visions we see spiritually through the Third Eye* happen less and less. This teenage time period was about remembering what I already knew. When I asked, "Who is this man?" someone said, "That's John-Roger." Who was this man? He had shown up when I was younger, then again in my late teens. I began to sense a connection with him at that moment. It would become a milestone for me to let me know I was "on course."

The qualities of the Spiritual Warrior began to percolate inside of me and I began seeking them.
1. "Love." What was true Love for me? Loving unconditionally.
2. Confidently making choices. A Hero. A Leader. To be clear in my choices.

3. Focusing my internal attention, even when the external realities of my everyday life were chaotic, troublesome, or just plain annoying. Focusing on my Inner guide.
4. Knowing the Inner and Outer worlds in awareness.
5. The courage to see myself, God, and Truth.
6. Family / Fellowship.

When I had seen the picture on the mantel, I saw what I wanted, but I could not see how to get it. I was hungry for it, for sure. I felt love beaming out of that photo. I wanted to know that man. Love was beaming in that seminar with David Hubbard. I was obsessed with the purple pattern, vapor-like essence that had eluded me for years, from the age of 13 through my teens. At night in my room, a purple ring would start off as a little dot, and then its diameter would grow to a burning purple sun pattern. It would pulsate on the right side and be elusive; when I tried to focus on it and bring my attention to it, it would go away.

I wanted love and family for sure in my life. I wanted to be courageous in seeing all, including the light and dark of who I am, and the Purple. It took another seven years, when I was in my early twenties, to discover that the Spirit-Man was John-Roger. This experience was the Landmark of my life. It made a diamond-cutting impression into my Soul forever.

*As you journey along the path
of spiritual enlightenment,
you may discover many, many misconceptions
about the "spiritual person."*

*The most basic factor of spiritual teachings is
that you are already spiritual.*

There is nothing you need to do to become that.

– John-Roger
From: The Way Out Book
(Source: www.lovingeachday.org)

Love—Listen—Live—Let Go.

– Jesus Garcia, D.S.S.

Heroes

ह्

I wanted to be a Hero. How could I be that Leader, that Spiritual Warrior, that Hero? How could I be that one to save the world? The one with the Superpowers? The Spiritual Warrior? It's important for me to note that my heroes throughout my life are many and have different qualities. Through my D.S.S. studies, I have come to know that each one represented some aspect of a Spiritual Warrior in me that I wanted to emulate; each one taught me more about being a Spiritual Warrior.

My first hero was, of course, my stepfather, who stood in as my father. My real father left my mother when I was born. They broke up, and I have no idea why. They never married. (Later I would meet him, at the age of 16, which was an interesting chapter in my life.) My stepfather stepped in, married my mother, and also had his own kids. He raised me, and he was unbelievable. He was a tough guy.

I do have a distant memory of a time before I was born. There was a black, dark void, maybe on another realm in Spirit, and there were men, or elders, which I surmise was a karmic board* somewhere. These men asked me if I wanted the tough father or the more sensitive father, and I said I wanted the tough father, the protector, the strength; and then *boom*, I was born in life somewhere in New Jersey, and that man was my stepfather. He was very tough: he looked a lot like the film character "Rocky Balboa." He was a mythical giant and my first hero. He loved his work and loved to travel; he was also a big womanizer, and no matter what the obstacles were, he almost always found a way around the problems, or he would solve it. (This would rub off on me because as an adult, womanizing would get me in trouble; and the traveling would later prepare me for traveling around the world with J-R.)

He did a lot of bad things. But what's interesting is that, as a child, I didn't judge him. It was only later that I really had problems with him for hitting my mother, fighting with her, and cheating on her. As a youngster, I fought back and told him what I didn't like. I would be crying while doing it. I think he found mercy for me because he stopped. But I loved him still. I loved him and I loved my mother. That, to me, was a very heroic time. It still felt like a family. He was my first hero because he took care of my mother and another man's child, me, during the tough times. He was a hard-working man. He brought home the bacon for Mom. There were moments when he would surprise me, and he'd grab me by the neck and throw me in the truck and off we would go like Odyssean adventures. We went all over the Eastern U. S., doing things together, and it was beautiful. He exemplified the quality of family for me.

My stepfather's courage was to express love to me by taking me with him on trips and teaching me about life on the road, how to have strength, how to do things even if it was hard at the time, through rain, snow, wind, or sun. He passed away a few years ago, and I noticed that when I heard he passed away, my own confidence got stronger. I became a man, a hero-in-training. Many heroes would follow after my stepfather.

I knew from a very young age that I wanted to be a movie star, but I didn't know what that really meant until I heard and saw Dean Martin. That was the start of the performing mania that caught my eye early on. Man, I wanted to be him, singing to all the women in the world and making them cry. He was charming and always laughing. I wanted to laugh my life away, to laugh my pains away to nothingness.

Elvis Presley did something to me that I can't explain. He had looks, voice, loyalty, and courage. His loyalty was his honoring of his parents and Christ. He earned many Gold Albums from gospel singing. I think his love for his mother was also the trait of a Spiritual Warrior: family first. And Elton John showed me my wild side.

Later, when I became a teenager, the singing heroes turned into acting heroes. I set out to fulfill my goal. I said to God, "I want to be in *TV Guide*. I want to be like Scott Baio and be photographed in every teen magazine," and I did it. I made the *TV Guide* and many teen magazines.

I was trying to beat James Dean's movie record of starring in three movies before he died. I was younger than he was when I completed filming my three movies. Now what? I really thought I was going to be the next James Dean. I never became a James Dean, obviously, but I loved his quality of freedom to express in the films I saw him in. I wanted so badly to express freely like him. I wanted to be able to cry and express to my father my true feelings. James Dean also had the courage to risk, to give it all even if he died trying. To me, he exemplified these qualities of a Spiritual Warrior.

Then, there was Marlon Brando, the greatest actor ever. I thought Brando displayed power, sensitivity (as well as good looks), and was courageous as a civil rights activist. But I saw a different face in Brando later. The courage he had seemed to scare him. His life taught me to be aware of the choices I make because any life could take a tragic turn. He is like an angel at that gate of vigilance.

Robert Kennedy and John F. Kennedy were two men who sacrificed their lives so that we can live the lives we live now. John Kennedy displayed true courage. He wrote, and won the Pulitzer Prize for, *Profiles in Courage*, a book that revealed to me that JFK knew that he would have to dig deep for the final moments of his life, to give his life for the greater good.

Martin Luther King Jr. is another hero, another Spiritual Warrior. He won the Nobel Peace Prize. He was killed shortly after his greatest speech. Here's the end of his speech:

> *But it doesn't matter with me now. Because I've been to the mountaintop And I don't mind. Like anybody, I would like to live a long life. Longevity has its place. But I'm not concerned about that now. I just want to do God's will. And He's allowed me to go up to the mountain. And I've looked over and I've seen the Promised Land. I may not get there with you. But I want you to know tonight, that we, as a people, will get to the Promised Land. And I'm happy, tonight. I'm not worried about anything. I'm not fearing any man. Mine eyes have seen the glory of the coming of the Lord.*
>
> *– Rev. Martin Luther King Jr. at Mason Temple Memphis, TN, April 3, 1968*

I felt that King knew that he would not live long. I was moved that he had a passion, could lead with his heart, and had a love for equality. When he made the positive choices in the face of chaos, his reward was liberty in his consciousness and his Soul; it's clear to me he was in the Grace* and in the flow. He feared no one. I'm obsessed with this quality of knowing that I will die doing the

Lord's work. I'm curious about the mystery of the relationship that King and other great men had with God.

Mohammed Ali (the boxer formerly known as Cassius Clay) was the Greatest. If you look at his record, he took more hits in his life than he did in the boxing ring. He refused to fight a war at the height of his championship, and they stripped him of everything he had earned. He appeared to be down for the count. But his life is a parable and a lesson on endurance. He taught me endurance and charm. He fought back with words and laughter. He had a powerful faith in God, while others didn't understand him and judged him for not being mainstream. Mohammed Ali exemplifies traits of a Spiritual Warrior by his strength and truth as well as by his knowledge of Islamic teachings; he wouldn't allow himself to collapse for very long. And he maintained the peaceful way.

Ronald Reagan brought me a sense of confidence during my teen years. It sounds funny, but I felt he was standing in as a father figure while I was in school. I remember I dreamed that he would be shot. Months later at school, I heard over the intercom that he was shot. At that moment, I felt I had some kind of spiritual connection to those I loved.

Abraham Lincoln and Jesus Christ are my biggest heroes. I still can't understand their ultimate sacrifice. Maybe it's Love. Lincoln tried to keep the Union together, and he did it at the cost of his life. Christ resurrected and went into hell, "kicked butt," and connected the lower worlds with the higher worlds. He saved many Souls that were trapped somewhere in a place that was not so great. Man, that tops it. How do they get the courage to put their bodies on the line? Where do they get their powers? How do Heroes get anointed for that one moment? *I'm in.*

When I finally met John-Roger in 1986, I realized this was my Hero, Teacher, Spiritual Warrior, and Wayshower—the "One" I'd been looking for my whole life. And he was alive! Many of the others I've been talking about are dead, and God Bless them. Although I love them, their bodies are gone.

J-R is in my face and he is the real deal. I am learning from a real live Hero. This John-Roger, in all areas, is definitely just a fantastic leader, a great leader. He means what he says, and he says what he means. He's totally here for God, committed to God's will. You can trust him. He never lies. He tells me the brutal truth. He is the most insightful person I've known. He knows how to *flow* with Spirit. He has crystal clear intentions. He continues to give to others selflessly. He can give the answer to the question before I ask it. I've never seen him depressed, never seen him complain. When people attack him, he only responds to them with love. And I aspire to be such a man, such a Spiritual Warrior, a man who continually makes confident choices, focusing the internal attention when the outer is chaotic. Being *receptive* to Spirit is what these heroes do.

To be a Spiritual Warrior is to exemplify the courage, the unconditional loving, the highest form of loving, the focus, the clarity and Spiritual Awareness: This is the focus of my own personal journey. This is the subject of this Treatise.

*We learn nothing by fretting
and becoming impatient.
We don't grow.*

*As Spiritual Warriors
we want growth and expansion.
So we observe.*

– John-Roger
From: Spiritual Warrior:
The Art of Spiritual Living
(Source: www.lovingeachday.org)

When you go forward, and you are giving the message of the light, The Mystical Traveler will go with you and transmute all karma, but as long as we stay within that framework the Sugmad has issued forward through The Mystical Traveler that we know can lift, and we put this out, no karma comes your way, you are giving forth the grace of God through your own beingness, we are the instruments in this physical level, now that we know let us become more perfect instruments on this level by more perfectly changing and adjusting to everyone that comes to us and then we have loved our neighbor as we have loved our God.

– JOHN-ROGER, D.S.S.
EXCERPT FROM *MYSTICAL TRAVELER* FILM

Finding My Outer Spiritual Warrior and J-R

हू

From very early in my life, I went in search of love, Spirit, and God. Although I didn't know it, I met people that knew people to help me get what I needed. Being young and caught up in the glamorous world of the movies, the wild life of drugs and promiscuous sex set in. I found the right acting agent, and I went to acting classes: I studied. I got involved in the materialistic things in the world while feeling a tremendous emptiness inside. I would do the drugs and numb myself, avoiding my true feeling that this wasn't working for me. Afterwards, I just felt this hole, this vacuum, and I didn't know how to fill it. I tried to fill it with women, with drugs, with the desires of acting in films. I would do a movie, which I thought was going to be the ultimate high, the ultimate accomplishment, the completion of what I set out to do. Then I realized, "Wow, this is it? There's got to be more to life than this." I drifted away from who I was. With all the acting roles I did and all the women, I lost myself. I lost my identity. I was living the life of an actor and not the life of a human. Me.

Insight Seminars (a series of personal growth seminars, founded by John-Roger in 1978) was in my peripheral sights; I kept running into David Hubbard who was still making movies, still going to acting classes and doing the Teen Insight Seminars. I thank God David was the beacon to remind me of that one moment in that house when I first met him: to come back home to what I really wanted. Insight Seminars is a fantastic, Heart-Opening training. All through the 1980s, these Insight Seminars were all the rave and are still ongoing today. I had people around me, saying, "You need to take Insight Seminars," and eventually I did; after that, I stopped the drugs pretty fast.

I was dating a girl at the time (who will remain anonymous), and I told her, "You need Insight." It was my way of blaming her for the relationship not working. We broke up, mostly because what I was looking for wasn't in her. It was inside of me. She took the training and it changed her life. Me? I soon dropped off the face of the earth, and off the wagon. I remember I walked on fire with Anthony Robbins around the same time because Robbins was in the same building as Insight Seminars. When I finished the Fire Walk (which, by the way, I did four times), I got bored. I wanted more. And then she found me, helped me get sober, and brought me back to life again. She saved me by encouraging me to take Insight Seminars again, which I did: Insight I and II, back-to-back trainings in 1987. It would be my first time to do Insight II. It was just the most incredible training I've ever taken. I wanted to go deeper. For me, it was 10 days of love. It's more powerful if you do the trainings back to back. It changed my life. I was in love after that training.

I wanted love. I wanted to know what love would be like in a real relationship. I think, during the whole time before Insight, I was just not realizing what love was. I thought love was, "Take your pants off and let's do it, baby," and it wasn't. It was way more than that. I wanted to know this unconditional love that everyone was alluding to. Movies and music and friends were showing me love, but I wasn't getting it. Then, after my Insight I and II, I wanted to conquer the world.

I remember choosing to keep my word about doing a movie, which consequently meant I couldn't participate in a Steven Spielberg movie. I went off to Colombia to do this other movie that I had given my word to do, and I remember praying to God, "I want to fall in love. Show me love." This relationship with "God / Inner-Guide" in prayer was gaining strength inside me. The more sober I became, the more the connection to God opened and became clearer to me. I met a girl on the set of my film. I fell off the wagon again, but I also fell in love with this girl, who later became my wife. The love I felt at that moment was a quality of a Spiritual Warrior. I wanted to feel it in my reality. The altitude allowed me to make the right choices and reach an awareness I never had before. And I still felt empty. Why? I became afraid and lost my courage, and I fell into darkness with drugs; and I kept finding ways to make believe this wonderful experience never happened.

A friend who had taken the Insight I and II with me two months before the film, gave me half a dozen John-Roger books to read while on location shooting. I knew this was what I wanted, but at the same time I had a drug addiction, and I was filming in the middle of Colombia, the Mother Lode of Cocaine. I was afraid of losing myself. There was a lot of pain inside me wanting to come out of my guarded heart. I wanted to create the family I never had but I thought I had to give everything up to Spirit in order to be spiritual. (Twenty years later, I came to realize I didn't have to give anything up; I just had to watch not to be attached to anything. I first had to find the discipline within my heart, and it would happen. I learned that I can use things while I'm here;

I just can't own them. I was awake, and once I awoke I could not turn back.)

After playing around in Colombia with my wife-to-be, and the drug addictions, I decided to come home, buckle down, and start reading the Soul Awareness Discourses, these little booklets that are given every month by MSIA. My relationship wasn't filling the hole I had. And I began, every month, having these incredible experiences. John-Roger has conducted seminars for his students for over 45 years, and the recorded tapes, called Personal Seminar Tapes, are available through MSIA. I engrossed myself in these tapes, and I was just blown away by this man and what he had to say. I also realized the tapes tend to take one to a more meditative state. They helped me to relax. When one relaxes, the consciousness is more available for spiritual experiences. I found this to be uncomfortable and fearful. I preferred to listen to them consciously, so I would drive around for miles and hours and oversaturate myself with these tapes. The information on the tapes became familiar. The knowledge I already knew, but I still needed the *awareness* of the Spirit that was enhanced by listening.

I was struggling to keep the marriage going. Everything was fine, but the true Love was missing. Once I tasted of the spiritual love, the higher love that I was not finding in the marriage, I knew I had to sacrifice one or the other. The two could not live together. I saw my path was one direction, and she was on her own path. The two paths didn't meet. The emotions were there, but the loving moved. Being married was beautiful, but I had all the Catholic guilt: "I cannot fail in this marriage; oh no, the guilt." "I am a Catholic! Oh, NO!"

I had issues with my mother, and I began to see the metamorphosis inside my wife or what I was projecting, at least. And all the "Daddy / Husband" issues were coming out in me. I came to the conclusion that my relationship was about what "role" I could play in this relationship with this woman, and what part could she play to fulfill me? What were each other's fantasies? I didn't know how to love myself and to be myself in a relationship. I was too busy playing some role that I never got to fulfill. Maybe that's what a first marriage is about?

I ended up making more movies while trying to keep the relationship going, and I must give credit where credit is due. It goes to my wife. In trying to keep my relationship with her, I took a training that John-Roger was offering at the time called The Relationship Seminar, based on J-R's book, *Relationships: The Art of Making Life Work*. The seminar was held at the Sheraton Universal in 1987, and that, again, changed my life. It helped in terms of my relationship with myself first, and that was a key. I decided to commit to Spirit 100 percent.

I did have my first encounter face-to-face with John-Roger during the seminar / workshop. I raised my hand and was chosen to share. Before I shared, he walked up to me and said, "What's your name?" I said, "Jesus Garcia." He said, "No, Spirit's telling me something else." I said, "Nick Corri (which was my stage name)." He said, "That's it." And I just lit up, to be recognized by the Spirit-Ghost Man. I knew I'd known him for a long time. It's hard to explain, but there are people in this world that I will always know somehow, somewhere, for the rest of my life, many lives, and eons.

I shared at that workshop that I would like to work with John-Roger. I didn't even think about it; I just said it. I wanted to be like John Morton, who was then, and still is, his right hand and works with him very closely. I was so high that day. I had met the man, the Spiritual Warrior, the Mystical Traveler, my old friend. I started to read about trips that J-R led throughout the world, and I saw a promotional video on J-R's travels. The trips were called, "Peace Awareness Trainings," or "PAT IV"; their focus was to teach people how to bring a focus of loving and peace to all areas of the world and, most of all, inside oneself.

I was reading the *Relationships* book one night by candlelight. I began falling asleep after reading a chapter in the book; the candle next to the bed, which I let burn in the evenings at bedtime, burned half the book (instead of my mattress and my shaggy rug). I could have been dead. I woke up in the early morning and saw the book burning; I threw some water at it and put out the small fire. Apart from it not being fireproof, it was a fantastic book, filled with tips on unconditional loving, tips to basically become a Spiritual Warrior for myself and my wife. The book was talking to me. It was teaching me to take responsibility for my actions and not to blame my wife. I didn't need to lean on her or smother her but love and care for her unconditionally.

We tried, but I guess I didn't really want the relationship, because I wanted to be free. I had given up on getting her to do what I wanted to do. She was free, and I needed to be free too. I would plan something, but I needed to always consider her when I wanted to do something spontaneous. I had never liked that part of a relationship. I wanted to be free to do what I wanted. I needed to change everything.

I scored a great acting job in New York, a beautiful role in a film and a beautiful experience. I ended up getting a job with Merchant Ivory on a movie called "Slaves of New York"; I went to New York, and I brought my wife with me. It was nice for both of us.

I started to see many miracles happen. I was in James Ivory's office when I got the news that I got the part, and I ran and danced in the streets of New York. As I passed a TV store, on one of the television sets I saw the music video from Michael Jackson's "Man in the Mirror." Wow. This song was deep; it hit me hard and I cried for two blocks. Part of the lyrics are, "I'm going to make a change, for once in my life." At that point in my career, I had dropped everything in order to get clean from drugs. Unfortunately, when I went for getting clean in my life, and that meant drugs and alcohol, I had to drop some friends that seemed like friends at the time but really weren't in the long run. They were just somehow enabling me, but I'm not blaming them; I take full responsibility. I dropped the bad influences. My wife helped me a lot, so we went forward. When I let go of control, I ended up getting better films.

So I was staying sober and watching my career change. I wouldn't say it went down. It just took a different turn that felt like it was in line with my Soul's progression. "Taking care of myself" became the number one priority. I was so hungry for the Spirit after all those years of not taking care of "me," and not learning about "who I am," "where I come from," and "what life's all about."

John-Roger and his staff happened to be in New York during the time I was shooting the film. I got a note to him inviting him to come to the set and visit me. John-Roger came with his assistant, and I was blown away. I wanted to work with him, but I didn't know how. I wanted to protect him and be his friend. I was in this acting world, but I was looking at this other life that I really wanted. I didn't think I could do it. I didn't think I could be part of that life. J-R already had plenty of people working with him. We talked. In J-R, I saw my Teacher after so many eons, my Wayshower. I had finally found him. What could I do?

One night after shooting, I was in a taxi with some actors and I was headed to a club where there would be women and beer. My wife was at home. I knew that night could be trouble. We passed the Sheraton Hotel, which is where J-R and his staff were staying. I yelled, "Stop the taxi," to the taxi driver. The guys were upset. I got out and went to a pay phone, and I called J-R's room. When he answered, he said my name. He knew I'd call him. We talked for a couple of hours. Man, I was on fire after that talk. I realized I had the chance of a lifetime to travel with J-R to the Middle East. I let him know that I wanted to go on this PAT IV trip. So I raised the money. My great friend OD gave me a loan. I will never forget him. When I finished shooting, and Merchant Ivory Films finally paid, I paid for my trip in full and paid OD back. I gave my wife a bunch of money, and I said, "Let's just go our separate ways, and I'll see you when I see you." She said, "Fine, I'll stay in New York," and away I went to my first PAT IV trip.

On Lufthansa Airlines en route to Egypt, I sneaked into the First Class cabin and knelt down next to John-Roger and just cried. I just felt something happening. I had finished two years of Soul Awareness Discourses, twenty-four of the little books, and I had made my request for my first initiation.* Before I received my first initiation, I had to be tested, and I was.

John-Roger led our group to the Middle East. There were about 150 people on the trip. After a stopover in Amsterdam, we flew into Cairo, Egyp, the next day, then took an overnight train to Aswan. In the dining section of the train, we all gathered and danced to Egyptian music. We arrived in the morning in Aswan, boarded the river cruise ship and began the journey towards Alexandria.

We cruised on the Nile River on an Egyptian cruise ship; we did meditations, visited temples, and listened to John-Roger share with us about life and Spirit, all while cruising and drinking hibiscus drinks. We entered the Promised Land—Israel—through Mount Sinai. We soon entered Jerusalem and saw the old city and went to the Galilee Kibbutz called Nof Ginosar. We saw all these beautiful biblical places; we saw the Dead Sea and climbed Masada, which blew my mind away. I learned from the vastness of God's deserts. In the desert my mind was really loud. I heard all my junk and it was amplified, too. Climbing Mt. Sinai seemed never-ending, a mountain that almost continued into the heavens. I can't explain it adequately. I had found the outer Spiritual Warrior, but I was also beginning to open to the Inner Spiritual Warrior.

Finding My Outer Spiritual Warrior and J-R

While we were on this pilgrimage, we had some studying to do. There were several books to read. One of them was Hermann Hesse's *Journey to the East*, as well as *Initiation by the Nile*, by Mona Rolfe and, of course, the MSIA Soul Awareness Discourses.

The pilgrimage to these holy sites changed my view of the world early on. These trips expanded my mind and Soul. I started thinking beyond me, beyond who I thought I was. The Spirit blew me away, especially when I heard J-R speak to me. *Star Wars* had been a life-changing movie for me when I was 17 years old. I wanted to be a Jedi Knight. I resonated with the characters "Yoda" and "Obi Won Kenobi," and their words spoke to me in the film *The Empire Strikes Back*. Listening to J-R was as if Yoda was talking to me. In a sense, *Star Wars* prepared me for the Spiritual Warrior's way. Yoda spoke of traits in *Star Wars* that are the qualities of the Spiritual Warrior's way: "Do or do not ... there is no try." "Named must your fear be before banish it you can." The wisdom, the clarity, the down to earth, ordinary, magnificent teachings from J-R were opening my receptivity to Spirit. I felt the grace and love emanating towards me.

I loved it. We went to every tomb and temple known to man. The temperature seemed like 120 degrees. I immediately gravitated towards John-Roger and I went everywhere he went. On that trip, I became a part of his traveling staff. I had no clue what I was getting into but, man, I loved it. The energy was a blazing fire of Light. I got to hang out and watch how he worked with the staff, and how he shared, and it was beautiful. Then we entered the Promised Land, and I remember Israel was gorgeous. Israel was like going home.

As the trip was ending, John-Roger and his staff and a small group were going to Russia and Germany. I wanted to go on this trip. John-Roger asked if I'd like to go and I said, "Yeah," because I didn't want this dream to end. He told BD, the travel coordinator, to slot me in, and Bam! Off we went to Russia and Germany, and in Germany, everything came to a halt for me emotionally. I was in pain, and I really missed my wife. I was sad most of the time. I realized I had crossed the line. I had crossed the line of no return. This spiritual movement that was happening inside of me was so strong and powerful. It felt like, as a newly bitten human, I was longing to finish the transition into a Vampire. Once I tasted the Spirit I could not turn back. It was a tidal wave that could not be stopped, not by a relationship, not by a marriage, not by a career, and not by anything. The dam was about to break.

I called my wife from Germany. I emotionally needed her back. I was still in love with her. I said, "I miss you. I really want you." I begged her. "I'll fly back right now, right now, if you tell me you love me and we're back, just tell me you love me," I pleaded. I heard a long pause on the telephone line, and I realized that was it. The dam broke. She was really sticking to her guns, and I realized it was over. I dove into the depths of sadness and Spirit's awakening. If that was my test, I passed the test, but man it was HARD to move forward.

On the train to Leningrad and St. Petersburg (or Stalingrad), I received my first initiation, and that was an amazing experience. I would say that my greatest initiations have been on trains, in hotels, and in exotic lands around the world. I definitely will never forget that 1988 PAT IV trip.

When I returned home, I had to go back to do re-shoots, to finish making *Slaves of New York*. I also served my wife the divorce papers. It took maybe three to five years to completely "cut the tail" on the relationship. That's what John-Roger used to tell me, and still tells me—"Cut the tail of the dog." Otherwise, if you cut the tail off a little at a time, it's just so painful. But with one fast cut—slam—you never have to deal with it again. The divorce was difficult and painful. The pain was still there, but sure enough it eventually went away.

Finding My Outer Spiritual Warrior and J-R

One of the things I love the most is music. In my mind, so much of my love for my wife was tied to hearing certain songs. Any song I would hear had an emotional memory, and I found I couldn't enjoy music. It was just too painful. It took me years to desensitize myself to that music, to relearn the music and fall in love with music again, and to attach new inner objects to the music. I never saw my wife again. God bless her for helping me stay on track. A new chapter in my life was about to begin.

Clean of drugs, clean of everything—it was just like a rebirth. I began my training with John-Roger, with the Spiritual Warrior. To me, it was like living in the movie *Star Wars*. I was Luke and J-R was Obi Wan Kenobi. I returned to Los Angeles and began living and working with John-Roger in the fall of 1988 as a member of his personal staff.

At MSIA's annual Conference in 1988, John-Roger had passed some of the keys of the Mystical Traveler Consciousness to John Morton, another staff member, and by the fall of 1988 it would be confirmed. J-R had held those keys for 25 years, and many of his students seemed to interpret his passing the keys to John as a sign that he would not be doing the work in the same way—that he would not be as active as a teacher and wayshower. John Morton stepped in to serve and help J-R with the work. From my observations, J-R continues to be active, and by example leads us all to the truth and the love that we already are.

I felt a desperate need to learn everything J-R taught. I thought I was going to lose him. In living with him, I learned so much, and really quickly. And so much discipline: "Say what you mean; mean what you say," I heard. "Just the facts, not your emotions, not your speculation, not your assumptions." I did a lot of meditations. It seemed like my spiritual lessons began in places I would never have thought. I began my lessons while driving J-R. I tried to be the best student, but I sometimes think I failed at that. I have no doubt J-R held me up from falling. I still think that.

We traveled around the world with him to different seminars, PAT trainings, Peace meetings, and Grace Retreats. Many people worked with J-R, one-on-one. I was privy to a lot of personal information and personal learnings people would have. I witnessed many one-on-one miracles right in front of me. And the interesting thing is, just because I live with a master, a Spiritual Warrior, doesn't mean that he's constantly "on," teaching me. No. My life with John-Roger mostly has been a strong friendship. When I was worse off, he was at his best. He was definitely with me during my painful divorce with my wife. Boy, I was crying all the time. That's part of being a Spiritual Warrior, to be able to cut anything that's not the truth with the sword of truth. My heart is my truth and my inner endurance, but the emotions would just kill me. J-R would say, "Your emotions lie; your mind and feelings are not you." He would say, "That's your ego," and his statement blew me away, because most of my other friends would pat me on the back and feel sorry for me and tell me what I wanted to hear. J-R is ruthless in his truth to me. J-R's core strength holds for him during adversity! He never speaks ill of anyone. His receptivity to Spirit, his blunt statements, his courage, and his unconditional loving exemplify the Spiritual Warrior's traits and qualities.

Ancient Man in PAT IV

Being with the Traveler, with John-Roger physically, is like being with a walking encyclopedia of sacred teachings. One of the great moments I remember from the PAT IV trip was encountering Ancient Man.

In 1988, at Nof Ginosar Kibbutz in Israel during my first PAT IV, John-Roger at times would be "out of the body" meditating, working in the inner realms, and there would be another person, an ancient being, an ancient man, that would be present, protecting his body. It was a caretaker, a guardian if you will, to guard his body while J-R Soul traveled to realms and levels beyond the physical. In order to do his spiritual work, J-R actually has to detach from the body and travel spiritually. On that first Pat IV trip, while I was eating in the cafeteria (Kosher, of course, I couldn't mix the dairy with the meat), I was hanging around J-R and having fun getting to know him. He walked over to the meat side of the Kosher Cafeteria, and I reached out to say hello. He said, "Who are you?" in a different voice, in a different manner, like an ancient man. I didn't understand. I thought he was playing. He wasn't. It was my first encounter with this guardian, this old man—I call him the "Ancient Man." The Ancient Man has abilities; he has incredible talents. One of them is that he is able to see through me, through things, and to see microscopically. When I grabbed his attention, other staff members were there helping, and they told me, "Don't touch him." The Ancient Man remembered me, and he smiled. He looked at the glass of water that I was drinking from, and he said, "Wow, that water is dirty." In fact, at the time, I didn't know what he meant, but when I put the water to the sun, I could see the particles in there, and it was really dirty. There was no physical way for this old man (or John-Roger) to see the particles in the water because it was not in front of the sun, and it looked like clean, crystal-clear water. The Ancient Man can be like a baby seeing things for the first time. When I first moved in and began working with John-Roger, and over the many years of working with J-R since then, I have met this Ancient Man many times since. He is a friend. He's really fun to be with, and he can read me like a deck of cards. I've never had anything to hide from him, so he was a blessing to get to know, and God bless him, wherever he is.

Living With a Spiritual Warrior

Although I live with a Spiritual Master, daily, and I have access to that Spiritual Warrior, I have come to know I also have access to my Inner Master. I notice that whenever I'm working on a film or a TV show, the spiritual information from my Inner Master, is louder, stronger than if I were physically with J-R. And that's really the experience of living with the Spiritual Warrior. The connection and the discernment that I feel with any kind of information, what I'm processing in my life, always bring a clarity about what my next steps are. I began to realize that the awareness to make the right choice brings me closer to the Inner Guide,* and it gives me a joyful result.

In our travels, I noticed that the people that J-R met, touched, shared with, and influenced seemed to have gone away with something more powerful—some Light, some blessings. I think that's what a Wayshower does. That's what he does as a Spiritual Warrior: he blesses people, places, things, good or bad, regardless of situations, circumstance, or environment. I've seen many miracles. I was in East Berlin with J-R when he prayed that the Wall dividing East and West Berlin would come down. And in one year the Wall came down.

When I looked at the Wall at the time, I did not see how this would happen, but it did. It's one of the miracles of God.

One of the greatest things I've gotten to experience while living with a Spiritual Warrior is getting to meet many people like Mikhail Gorbachev and Raisa, his wife, in Moscow; we met him again in El Paso, after Raisa passed away. We met Al Gore when he was a Senator; we met Bill Clinton. Before I came on staff, J-R had met many great giants of our time.

When John-Roger steps forward, when he touches people, they change. The flow and love that emanates from J-R changes things. In the 1980s, he had an organization that gave Integrity Awards, celebrating and honoring the recipients during Integrity Day, September 24, which is J-R's birthday. These awards went

Finding My Outer Spiritual Warrior and J-R

out to people like: Stevie Wonder, Oliver Stone, Mother Theresa, and Desmond Tutu—really great people who were demonstrating integrity. I remember one recipient, the Polish poet, Lech Walesa, who later became president of Poland.

J-R met Pope John Paul; J-R and I met Armand Hammer, who was one of the richest guys in the world. The reason I'm name-dropping is that it's a good thing to meet these people and to have contact with many people, not just these influential people. I believe the Spirit rubs off on all of us when we come in contact with each other. For example, at the height of the first Gulf War, Mu'ammar al-Qaddafi, Libya's military ruler since 1969, came to Cairo with the Arabs for a meeting to decide on Saddam Hussein's fate. Coincidently, Qaddafi was staying at the same hotel we were staying in. We sent him Light and love and peace at the time.

The bottom line is that J-R's influence seems vast to me. It's wonderful to see how the people he has met have changed the world. One might think it's a coincidence, but I think it is not. I believe John-Roger and the groups that he led through the Middle East for many years were influential in slowing down the wars and keeping them from escalating and getting out of hand. I believe in that energy. I believe and know that if enough people would think peace, enjoy traveling, loving and crossing borders, sharing and meeting people of different cultures, there would be more peace and less trying to blow things up. Jesus Christ told us, "Where two or three are gathered, there I shall be." (Matthew 18:20, NIV) Sending people or situations the Light as a Spiritual Warrior and praying for them creates miracles. I can be a Spiritual Warrior cell for peace. I am a "love cell" that multiplies. I seek to use all my talents as a Spiritual Warrior in my service to J-R.

When people ask me what a Spiritual Warrior looks like, I say, "Just like you." It is what you are doing inside of you while you participate outside of you—a totally simple way of living, an internal harmony and balance. The Spiritual Warrior does not draw conclusions or take positions which then need to be defended.

– JOHN-ROGER, D.S.S.

Finding My Inner Spiritual Warrior

I thought my spiritual lessons would come by some "Parting of the Red Sea" way. They did not. John-Roger was my model. I saw him making the right choices that resulted in J-R being more receptive to Spirit. His choices came after he checked inside with his Guide. He has exemplified awareness by knowing to focus on the positive. Even when attacked, I've never seen J-R upset, emotional, or hurt. These are the qualities of a Spiritual Warrior. As I have worked with him, he has allowed me to grow by falling and learning. He's never inflicted his truth on me, but rather has allowed me to find my own truth. That is love. He transmits love, and it's contagious. He gives me the freedom to learn. J-R has taught me many things about being a Spiritual Warrior.

*As you cut through the waste matter of your life,
you may feel resistant and uncomfortable;
you may be spacey, sleepy, antsy or distracted.
Never fear.
Someone once said, "If you don't feel awkward
doing something new,
you are not doing something new."*

– John-Roger
From: Spiritual Warrior:
The Art of Spiritual Living
(Source: www.lovingeachday.org)

Finding My Inner Spiritual Warrior

Driving J-R

One very important way of learning spiritual lessons was driving. I drove for J-R and still drive for him today. I would say the most important thing that I loved, and still love, about my relationship with John-Roger is driving him in a car. Driving him anywhere in the world. Driving the car, taking the lead, learning how to drive. I learned simple things such as finding out how many gallons of gas are being used per hour; how to send the Light ahead on the road and ask for protection from God; how to drive smoothly so as not to wake J-R from his meditation. My life is about the car. My biggest lessons come from driving. Control is a sacred cow of mine. Driving taught me to watch how I'm addicted to control. To this day, I still wear out my brake pads. J-R keeps telling me to slow down, or how to drive with more awareness of my surroundings on the road, and for some reason, I still go unconscious mostly when I drive by myself.

Driving is a great metaphor for life, really. In my D.S.S. Individual Study of living the life of a Spiritual Warrior, one of the areas I chose as a focus was the quality of Awareness. Checking awareness is key in driving. Am I paying attention, being aware? Or am I going unconscious and forgetting the off-ramp that I should have taken? Should I have gotten out of that lane? Am I putting my blinkers on and letting people know where I'm going? Or am I just going unconscious? Am I day dreaming? Am I not in the present? Am I blasting my high beam headlights onto the faces of oncoming drivers? I am. Am I "flipping the bird" at my fellow human being? And I am. So, it is definitely quite a learning experience.

Horses

I learned more lessons while riding horses. MSIA has a ranch in Santa Barbara. I would drive J-R up there every weekend beginning in 1988. The drive was about two hours each way. We would drive to Windermere Ranch and ride horses with John-Roger and friends. He taught me the way of the horses. The way I act around a horse really tells me a lot about myself, and the horse reflects it back to me. When I rode horses with J-R, I learned how to talk to animals, how to touch them, how to let them feel relaxed around me. If I am tense, they are tense. If I give them confused signals, then they give me confused signals. Once J-R told me to ride up the sheer rock, which was at a 45 degrees slant. He told me not to be afraid. I was, but I went for it. As I reached the top my horse slipped under me and rolled over me. I felt fear, thus the horse felt my fear, and we fell. I thought I broke something. J-R walked over to me and touched me and I felt no pain; he told me to get back on the horse and do it again. This time he went first and he made it, which gave me the courage to go for it. I did. I made it up the hill. He taught me right there and then: When you get knocked down, get up. Get back on the horse. If I hadn't, I know it would have killed my confidence. This lesson still helps me today. If I get rejected from an acting job, I get up and go for the next acting job. The hurt is less and less there, and it is a much shorter time to get over it.

Losing My Walkie-Talkie

I remember another instance of how things became magical for J-R and me. I had been working more and more closely with him with regard to listening, minimizing ego, and flowing with the Spirit. We were riding at Windermere Ranch one day. Windermere once was the land of the Chumash Indians; it is about 140 acres, a huge piece of land, and a very mystical land. We were using walkie-talkies to communicate with one another. On this particular day, I dropped my walkie-talkie somewhere; after riding with J-R for over an hour, I couldn't find the walkie-talkie. So J-R said, "I didn't hear the walkie-talkie fall on the ground; maybe it fell in the pond. Check the pond." The pond was man-made, and the water was about four feet deep. I would have to be in the water chest high if I were to start looking for the walkie-talkie. But even if I had dropped it in this huge pond, how would I know where? I needed to move quickly because the water would damage the walkie-talkie.

John-Roger said, "Go to the pond, and I'm going to start talking on the walkie-talkie." And I'm thinking, "How will I hear it? It would be underwater." But, unbelievably, John-Roger clicked his walkie-talkie and said, "Breaking for Zeus. Breaking for Zeus!" (My nickname is Zeus.) And I saw bubbles popping up to the surface of the pond. And I was thinking, *No way!* It was just crazy, unbelievable. I went into the pond, chest-high, and put my hand down to where the bubbles were coming from, and I pulled out the walkie-talkie. (That was one of many Spiritual Warrior moments.) J-R taught me in that moment to flow and to not let my ego override the listening that goes on inside. I really learned about *awareness* that day. I also began to learn to listen to the Inner Master* or Guide.* I started to become receptive.

*If we can change our spiritual consciousness,
we can move toward the convergence point.
We can spend more of our time
in spiritual pursuit
instead of just reacting to the material world.
We can remain at peace.
We can never control God,
but we can align and flow with His will.*

– JOHN-ROGER
FROM: SPIRITUAL WARRIOR:
THE ART OF SPIRITUAL LIVING
(SOURCE: WWW.LOVINGEACHDAY.ORG)

The Travels of a Mystical Traveler

घू

Dreaming of a Spiritual Warrior

Dreams have become an indication to me that I am receptive to Spirit. When I am in my ego, when I am not in flow with Spirit, I tend not to remember my dreams. When I remember my dreaming, I know I am more in flow and more aligned with my Inner Spiritual Warrior and my life is more graceful.

In 1994, J-R, John Morton, and I went scouting around for the route of the next PAT IV trip, which would be another pilgrimage to the Middle East. We went to Jordan, Syria, and Lebanon, as well as Israel and Egypt. That trip was marvelous, incredible. Before we arrived in Syria, I had done a lot of reading about the

Mesopotamian period and the Peloponnesian Wars. And I began having reincarnation dreams; one of the things I dreamed of was Queen Zenobia.* I dreamed of a beautiful Roman city called Palmyra, which is still there today (in ruins but preserved). It felt like Syria was dreaming me, dreaming me about that ancient lifetime. The trip found us meditating while on the bus, rolling down the highway, feeling free and flowing with the Spirit. I was flowing and aligned with Spirit. I experienced myself in the circle of Light, another indication to me of being in the flow. I never felt "off"; I was in the flow. I experienced Grace. I felt I was caught in a spiritual vortex. Palmyra was where I received my next initiation. Years later we ended up using these locations in the movie, *Spiritual Warriors*. It was stamped into my consciousness, and I could never forget these places.

On these trips, experiences can come and go so quickly, and they can be erased. They tend to be so fluid and so elusive; they almost feel like a dream. "Did it happen?" "Did it not happen?" They are quite unlike experiences of a negative or a karmic nature, which I tend to remember all day long. And that's when I started to realize these moments of being in flow, in grace, receptive to Spirit, are different types of experiences.

*Spiritual Warriors are trained
in the heat of adversity.
But you know something?
You're tempered by the Spirit of God.*

– John-Roger
From: Spiritual Warrior:
The Art of Spiritual Living
(Source: www.lovingeachday.org)

A Greek Death

In 1995 we traveled to Greece. This was a trip between two trips to the Middle East, but on this trip I found myself "acting up," acting out of ego, being out of alignment, out of flow. It was more like how not to be a Spiritual Warrior. Unlike the scouting trip with the Travelers, when I was really focused, on this trip I was not aligned and not in the flow, and I thought I knew everything about life. Just like most neophytes tend to do on their spiritual path, I blew it. I remember on the cruise ship eating some food and getting my tea leaves read by three hot, young girls. We called them the Greek Sirens, like in Homer's *Odyssey*. They told me I was going to die. I laughed and kept misbehaving. J-R warned me, "You're out of balance."

Later that night I began throwing up from both ends. I began dehydrating rapidly and dying quickly. I ended up in the hospital the next day and was diagnosed with salmonella poisoning. The poison had hit most of the passengers on the ship, an outbreak. And I was the worst. J-R was with me in the hospital, just there keeping me company. I felt he saved my life by providing continuous spiritual energy. He continues to save my life.

I had major hallucinations because of the high fever, and I remember J-R telling me to just go with it. I would say that I saw my own death in that time period, because I thought for sure I was going to die. I was very sad at the time; I thought, "Wow, is this the way I'm going to die? What a way to go. After all the things I've been through—I thought I was going to be like a hero, killed in the line of duty." This was not a heroic way to go. I was slipping into darkness. I gave up mostly because I knew J-R was by my side. I surrendered to God's will. I thought, "If I'm going to die, then I guess I can't stop it, so I might as well flow with it. Accept it. Drop the ego. Fly." I stopped fighting. Because J-R was by my side, I accepted my fate. I recovered four days later, and I was a different man. I thought, "I have to be careful what I say." When we had landed in Greece before I got sick, I remembered I had said inside to myself, "I could die here." Well, I almost fulfilled that statement.

Once I was able to travel, J-R and I headed back to Cairo and met up with John Morton and the PAT IV group. I had learned a lot. I became stronger. Definitely, I was humbled. I had had a conversion moment. Spirit had taught me about disillusionment. The inner worlds are more important than the outer. Seeking the Spirit first and learning to flow and trust the inner worlds are a priority. I learned not to be afraid of dying. I realized I needed to bring myself to an awesome awareness and to listen to my inner guidance.

My Practical Treatise is called "Living with a Spiritual Warrior." To me, it means living with myself, living with John-Roger, my Wayshower, and being aware of the choices I make that give me joyful results. On the Greek trip I had made choices that resulted in not so joyful moments. If nothing else, I was thinking that if I had a plan here on this earth, or in this life, as to why I came here, it would be: to be here for this moment, to protect J-R, to be able to watch over him, and to be chosen to step into that place of service. I'd be available if anything would arise (whether it did or did not). I want my life to be one of valor and honor. John-Roger told me a long time ago, "You can change your Vanity into Valor." Being an actor sometimes turns my vanity on at a high level. But I strive to stand here as just a servant. The lessons have not always been easy. But I look back and think, "Wow, it was worth it. It was worth it, to stand where I stand and do what I do."

These were really the keys that changed my life. I try not to collapse or fall apart as much anymore. I try to keep strong about my inner guidance, or guide, or J-R in my head, which I feel is very connected to the Christ and to the Holy Spirit.

Life's Challenges

The toughest time I ever had (beyond my divorce) was when John-Roger was hurt. He fell and seriously injured himself. It was a middle of the night rush to the Emergency Room, emergency surgery, a stay in the hospital, a significant recovery time. The most serious injury turned out to be his eye. In a nutshell, what this event taught me was to take command; that a person who needs help doesn't need the other person to be in drama mode but rather to be in leadership mode, to assist and help, without the energy and the chaos of, "Oh, my God, look what happened to him!" I learned to be direct and finish the mission, which is to assist and serve in loving.

While J-R was hurt, I learned to trust myself. I flowed with such a deep connection to Spirit and inner guidance. I'm not the same person that I was before J-R's fall. I experienced myself more fully as the Spiritual Warrior.

Doctor of Spiritual Science Program

One day, after many years with J-R, I was contemplating studying at Peace Theological Seminary for my master's and doctorate degrees in the Master of Spiritual Science and Doctor of Spiritual Science programs. I was intimidated by many of my friends, who had already put in three years for the MSS and five years in the D.S.S.. One night I prayed and asked God for the answer; I was asking for a sign. The next day I was driving J-R to breakfast, and he looked at me and said to my face, "Yes, it's okay to start studying for your doctorate." I looked in shock. I said, "Yes, J-R, thanks so much. I've been asking Spirit and I didn't get an inner answer yet." J-R replied, "I heard you. It's fine to study for your doctorate." That blew me away. So I went for it. It has been a big learning for me. I work for J-R, "the boss," so I wanted to prove to myself that just because I live with J-R and work with him didn't mean I would have an easy ride. I needed to prove to myself that I could live up to J-R's teachings, to walk the talk. I wanted to experience getting from PTS what I put into it.

J-R has always been in support of my getting an education. I had dropped out of high school, and I went to college for one day. When I started working with J-R, he supported me in getting my General Education Diploma. I felt such a load coming off my shoulders. J-R was right: when I educated myself and completed in my life, it gave me so much more self-esteem and space for more creativity. It's another important area of my P.T., which I chose to focus on: completion in my life and not letting projects fall into oblivion.

Jesus Christ is the spiritual head of the Church of the Movement of Spiritual Inner Awareness, and the Traveler's work through MSIA is based on Jesus' work. Jesus Christ made it possible for all people to enter the Soul realm, whereas before that time, this was available only to a few people. Soul Transcendence, the spiritual work that John Morton and I do, builds upon Jesus' work and makes it possible for people to be established in the Soul realm, traverse the twenty-seven levels above Soul, and to go into the heart of God.

– JOHN-ROGER, D.S.S.

The Class

हू

Peace Theological Seminary & College of Philosophy

The D.S.S. class each month has given me a framework to experience awareness and flow in the world. I got to become even more aware of what being a Spiritual Warrior means. I began to find in my Heroes the elements of Spiritual Warrior-hood. I completed three years of the Master of Spiritual Science program (MSS). I'm now in my fifth year of D.S.S.. My consciousness has changed every month, and I have tools that I can use to live more as a conscious Spiritual Warrior.

One requirement of these programs is being a minister in MSIA.* I was ordained* in 1988. Studying at Peace Theological Seminary & College of Philosophy (PTS) has allowed me to really discover more of myself. I got to take a look at the blessings brought forward in my ministerial Ordination.* My Ordination blessing is a map that gives me clues to align myself when I'm "off." In the blessing it says, "Words of wisdom may come forth," and I know they definitely do. If nothing else in my life, I'm a straight shooter, and when I shoot something, I've got to say it's really accurate. When I want to be "on it," it's really dead on. I think when I'm "on," when I'm "in the zone," and I have that Spirit shining on me, I'm definitely saying words of wisdom, especially to myself. One of the best things J-R has taught me is to never play a victim. I learned a long time ago that I have created everything in my life. I am the master of my life.

*Getting your intention clear
and anchoring it inside of you
is the essence of Spiritual Warrior-hood.*

– John-Roger
From: Spiritual Warrior,
The Art of Spiritual Living
(Source: www.lovingeachday.org)

You never will make a mistake, so long as you keep in mind to act simply as the Master's agent. Then let Him take care of all results which may follow.

– Huzur Maharaj Sawan Singh,
Spiritual Gems

D.S.S. Intentions

घु

In my Master's class I began developing the intentions, and the methods, that would prepare me for my Practical Treatise, "Living with the Spiritual Warrior." My intentions for the D.S.S. were specific in helping to keep my focus. Here is a description of how these worked for me:

The word "Delicious" was in my Ordination. (*See the full text of the Ordination and Blessing in Appendix I at the end of this Treatise.*) Delicious Loving, to me, is just what the word means: something that tastes and feels good and loving is synonymous. This feeling runs throughout the cells in my blood. I think that when those are happening in the physical, that's what I want. One thing that happens with my P.T. is within the five years, my intentions have developed and moved into a more workable program.

For my methods currently, I use:

(1) Physical Movement/Workout. This included weight training, yoga, and running. I noticed that if I work out or do movement physically, then I feel healthier, and I look better because I am thinner. I also found that Joy (Delicious) comes up, which

is an indicator that I'm on track in the physical. Being fit and healthy calls me to make positive choices and to hold the positive focus of a Spiritual Warrior.

(2) Completions. For me, procrastination is insidious. Procrastination has many times caused me to doubt myself and basically paralyze my creativity. I challenged myself to complete at least three things each day, then I could move out of my rigidity, my creativity flowed, and I would break out of my negative patterns. These are qualities of the Spiritual Warrior. CKT* has added completion for me at the end of the day. Checking throughout the day and clearing up what may be holding me back and by naming it, it clears up.

<u>Emotional Intention: Spiritual Awareness</u>: Instead of being emotionally drained and emotionally reacting to things, I am working to have greater spiritual awareness, the ability to look down onto something from far away, so that I can see the landscape and make decisions more accurately and more objectively than subjectively. For my methods, I used:

(1) Journal Writing. My experience has been that when I write in my journal asking for more clarity in dreams, then I have great dreams that guide my life in a positive direction. My dreams connect me to a truth that lives within me and a spiritual focus.

(2) Checking My Awareness. When I check for my awareness (Am I in Flow? Am I in Grace? Is my ego clear?), the choices I make are often the more positive ones.

<u>Mental Intention: Silent Listening/S.E.'s</u>: I wanted to just listen, without having a tape recorder or ranting going on in my head while someone else is speaking. I tend not to listen because I'm busy talking in my head about the next thing I'm going to say in response to them.

The method I chose was listening to my Inner Guide.* I saw that when I'm listening inwardly to my Inner Guide,* I am being receptive to Spirit's lessons, information, messages, and (my favorite) experiencing the Sound Current* while awake.

<u>Spiritual Intention: Alignment to Spirit</u>: When I feel Aligned to Spirit / J-R, I am connected; I'm jacked up; "in the Zone"—all of those words. I feel that I'm at one with the Universe, the Spirit, J-R, God, Christ, and I have conviction. I make confident choices like a Spiritual Warrior. The method I used was Doing Spiritual Exercises. I have found that if I am doing S.E.'s, my spiritual practice, chanting my initiation tone* or the HU,* then I'm in sync with the Spirit. Aligning with the spiritual authority that transcends my ego and all things in this world and beyond is the type of alignment I'm talking about.

When I align, it prepares me to enter into my loving, my freedom, my joy, and that creates a positive outcome in my inner and outer worlds. Then my creativity is in flow with God's plan. The world can happen and it doesn't need to change. When I improve my attitude, this action affects my positive choices, and they in turn affect my inner and outer worlds. My choices have a clear conviction. I know I'm on track at that moment. I'm in the flow and I'm in the Grace. I have clearer answers for my choices.

*Health/Wealth/Happiness, Abundance/
Prosperity/Riches, Loving/Caring/
Sharing and most of all Touching.*

– JOHN-ROGER, D.S.S.

Hypothesis

ह्

I made the following tentative assumptions for my Hypothesis in order to test to see if my methods were useful and working:

Physical Methods: Physical Movement and Completions: IF I workout or do movement physically, THEN I will feel and be healthier, and I will look better. IF I am completing at least three things each day, THEN I can move out of my rigidity, free up my creativity, and break my negative patterns.

Emotional Methods: Journal Writing and Checking Awareness: IF I write in my journal asking for more clarity in dreams, THEN I will have great dreams that guide my life in a positive direction. IF I check for my awareness (Am I in Flow? Am I in Grace? Is my ego clear?), THEN the choices I make will be positive ones.

Mental Methods: Listening to My Inner Guide/J-R: IF I'm listening to my Inner Guide, THEN I am being receptive to

Spirit's lessons, information, messages, and (my favorite) experiencing the Sound Current while awake.

Spiritual Methods: Doing Spiritual Exercises: IF I am doing S.E.'s, my spiritual practice, chanting my initiatory tone or the HU, THEN I'm in sync with the Spirit.

My Hypothesis

1. Taken all together: IF I am being positive and creative, in flow, being receptive to and in sync with Spirit, THEN I will be living the qualities of loving unconditionally, confidently making choices, leading, clear in my choices, focusing my internal attention, even when the external realities of my everyday life were chaotic, troublesome, or just plain annoying. I am focusing on my inner guide, and I'm having the courage to see myself, God, continuing enjoying my family and friends in fellowship as Spiritual Warriors.

Verily, verily, I say unto you, He that believeth on me, the works that I do shall he do also; and greater works than these shall he do; because I go unto my Father.

– John 14:12 [KJV]

*God is my infinite supply & large sums of money
Come to me quickly & easily, under Grace,
In the most perfect way, for the highest good
of all concerned.*

– JOHN-ROGER, D.S.S.

Designing My Individual Study

घू

In the D.S.S. class, I created an Individual Study to see if I could enhance my experience of Living with the Spiritual Warrior—My Inner Spiritual Warrior. I wanted to see if I could consistently live with more awareness, deeper dreams, more receptivity to Spirit, more attunement and alignment with the Traveler and the Master within me, living as the Spiritual Warrior.

Methods

<u>Workout</u>: I knew that when I was not physically active, when I didn't work out, everything that is positive, loving, and joyful about myself started to fade. Working out is part of my discipline to keep everything else on track. When I work out I feel more loving, more in sync, and more joy towards myself. When I take care of myself that way, I find I do the same to others.

Completing/CKT: A lot of my blessings have come from completing and clearing using CKT. Clearing through Controlled Kinesiology Techniques assists me to name the problem, then I can gain greater understanding. When I name the problem it gives me dominion over it. Living with my Inner Spiritual Warrior is clearing myself, so that I can be aligned with Spirit, so that I can lift to God. I knew that completing things in my life brings freedom to my creative life. I found that it brings more creative writing in my journal.

Journal Writing: I knew that writing in my journal would help me to reflect on my dreams and on my awareness. (See p. 67 for a description.)

Checking Awareness: I knew that when I would just stop and track my awareness, I would allow myself to course correct and to talk to J-R inside. When I am having an inner dialogue, the results are having a connection with Spirit and allowing the Spirit to tell me what It wants.

S.E.'s and Meditation: I knew that when I did my Spiritual Exercises, I was more receptive to Spirit/God. I had the awareness to make the positive choices. S.E.'s bring me spiritual wisdom. I knew that listening to my Inner Guide helps me make better choices. I knew that doing Spiritual Exercises helped me stay positive and aligned inside.

In/Out of Grace, Flow, and Ego: checking how the dreams are flowing. Checking in my awareness of Spiritual wisdoms usually works close to the Journal writing. Stopping at the moment to check in on my ego. Being in the flow is where Grace lives. Grace is sort of like the "Get Out of Jail Free" card, from the board game Monopoly. I knew that I was challenged to keep my ego in check, to stay in the flow. I knew that when I tracked my awareness and found I was in my flow, then I began having messages in the dream state. I would have clearer answers for my choices.

When tracking the above methods, which I called the "If," then I would track the results of which I, in turn, called "Then," the results of; (**Working Out, Completing, dreams/Messages in sync with Spirit, Receptive to Spirit, inner talk with J-R/Inner guide and Writing in the journal**). The measurements are on a tracking sheet that includes a scale of improvement of (HML): High, Medium, or Low. Each sheet has the seven days of the week. I began with ten printed sheets and added two more for fun.

I used this Individual Study as a scientific way of proving to myself, or testing, my methods and tracking results. The requirements were to observe and track various experiences over a period of ten weeks. Although I completed my ten weeks, I gave myself two more weeks. By the end of the ten weeks, I found I had evolved, and I continue to become more aware of these methods that are the tools for my upliftment.

The Twelve-Week Individual Study

I created an individual study, which tested my methods and provided me with information about how effective my methods were in creating a road map to Living with the Spiritual Warrior.

My scale on the graph, which breaks down the 12 weeks of the study, has a scale of 0 to 7, "7" being high, feeling great all around; of course, "0" is a very low score on my week.

Week 1: Grandmother and trips happened in that week. The score of 3 was the beginning of my Individual Study.

Weeks 2 and 3: Scaled up to 4 because I worked on an acting job for a television show called *Without a Trace*.

Weeks 3 and 4: I felt very aware and flowing on the 3_{rd} and 4_{th} week.

Week 5: This week was bad. I found I needed help. I did a lot of clearing with J-R and other practitioners.

Weeks 6 and 7: This was a highlight, with the "Spiritual Warriors" trip to Tel Aviv, Israel. This trip was much like the PAT IV trips, which I described earlier. This was an all-time high of "7." I definitely felt I was receptive to Spirit, flowing, and Grace, and I felt very strong inside listening to my Inner Guide. In this case I made the right choices and that brought me awareness.

Week 8: The 8th week was tracked as Black Week. My score was "0." I found I was running my ego, not flowing, out of Grace and not doing much movement.

Weeks 9, 10 and 11: I scored higher. I felt I got back in line. I began to lose weight and I found more flow in my life.

Week 12: My final week 12 was good at first, but then dropped back into ego.

Nevertheless, at the end of my Individual Study, I had many wonderful dreams of spiritual essence. And I became aware that my methods do provide me with a road map to get back to "Living with the Spiritual Warrior" (me, my spiritual self) when I fall back into ego or negativity.

The Spiritual Warrior must get this one intention very clear: "I'm keeping my eyes on You, Lord, only You."

– JOHN-ROGER, D.S.S.

*We cannot demand or assume that
life will take care of us.
That is taking a position.
People who get stuck on a position are frozen.
They are chained to their needs, their anxieties,
and their desire for gratification.
If you insist that someone is
supposed to do something for you,
you have chained yourself to that.
Do you want those chains for your lifetime,
breakfast, lunch, and dinner?
Spiritual Warriors do not fall into the trap
of making their gratification and security
depend on other people.
The Spiritual Warrior goes for freedom.*

– John-Roger
From: Spiritual Warrior,
The Art of Spiritual Living
(Source: www.lovingeachday.org)

Outcomes

धु

Awareness from the film *Spiritual Warriors*
Receptivity to Spirit's "Flow"
God's Flashlight on Me

*I*n the United Kingdom during the *Spiritual Warriors* screening in September of 2007, I was following my intuition, which has conviction in it, feeling in *sync* and *flow* with God's plan. I felt I was making the right choices and I had no doubts. I confidently made choices. This was a method of being aware of and present with my Inner Master. Then, when the job got done, the flashlight of Spirit, the spotlight moved away. I was off of my center and into my ego; it seemed as if I was sort of back-to-normal behavior, which is ordinariness, because I have to learn in that level. Then came all the doubts, all the jealousies, all the lusts, and all the addictions. "Take the trash out. Things are piling up." I was forgetting the loving and not doing the spiritual work. In that moment I had to listen, drop the ego position, and focus the *awareness* towards God to align myself again. This process humbled me and dropped me to my knees, pointing my eyes towards the sky and asking God/J-R for Grace.

The method for me is praying and writing those thoughts to God in my journal (see p. 67 for description).

But when this Light shines upon me, it's as if I'm in the Zone. The Zone, in my definition, is when I'm flowing and receptive to Spirit. When I'm at one, I'm attuned to the Spirit. I'm connected to the source. I call it The Christ/John-Roger. I can move mountains, I can take all the rejections in the world, and just laugh and love it all. That energy is really what I thrive for, what I crave everyday. Every time it leaves me, I think that it will never come back again. "Come back to me, just one more time," I beg.

While we were in the U.K., about twenty of us went into Paris on the Speed Train one afternoon to share the Light in Paris. It really brought back those days when John-Roger used to lead those trips to the Middle East, when 150 of us would broadcast Light and Peace everywhere we went. The trip into Paris was an amazing experience. I was really in the moment, and I was there with the Spiritual Warrior inside of me. I saw that when I make the right choices, it brings me to my loving.

How Dreams Guide Me

One of the ways I know I am living with my Spiritual Warrior is when my dreaming provides me a doorway into Spirit's guidance. Here is an example of this: I couldn't find my credit card, and John-Roger has a technique he calls "Reach." It calls upon the cooperation of the Basic Self, which is the consciousness that knows the details of many routine things we do in life: brushing the teeth, putting clothes on, getting the keys to the car in the kitchen, grabbing the wallet, money, and going for a drive. And the Basic Self tends to know where the credit cards are, and things like that. But this time I couldn't find my credit card. It's very rare that I lose anything. I'm a good finder of lost things also. This was bizarre. I had a feeling it may have been in the trash, because I checked inwardly. "Is it in the house?" I asked. "No," my Inner Guide said. Then I asked J-R, "What do you think? Is it in the house?" He's really good at this game. He said, "I don't see it in the house, but just say 'reach.'" I did go out to the trash but only picked up a few pieces. It was dark and dirty. I kept wishing and wanting it to be in the house, so I didn't have to do all that looking. My ego set in. I didn't allow the awareness of listening. I didn't let Spirit flow through me.

Before I went to sleep that night, I wrote in my journal, "God, please help. Please help me find the credit card." I'm abundant. I could have called and cancelled the card, but that's a hassle. For me, it was about finding the card, not giving up. I was praying in my head, "God, please, do something. Do something. Show me some power. Show me a sign." And that night I was blessed with a dream. God, Spirit talked to me in my dream. I felt the flow with Spirit. My awareness was on fire. In my dream I saw myself outside by the trash, grabbing a plastic trash bag, opening it, and then taking the trash out of it piece by piece, emptying it out. There were seven big buckets of trash, all with many trash bags.

When I woke up, I remembered the dream. I dreaded going out and going through the trash. My ego almost got in the way. However, I just accepted and flowed with the Spirit. I committed myself to doing it. I walked outside and began. I grabbed a bag, I pulled one, two, three pieces out of it, and I looked into the bag. There was my credit card, and I was shocked.

I just praised the Lord at that moment. I couldn't believe it. Then I realized that all I had to do was fulfill what the pictures in my dream were showing me, as closely as I could. I experienced this phenomenon. I knew I would find the credit card. This was a big indication to me that if I got a picture of something, a vision in my dreams, I needed to fulfill something of that vision. I knew that if I did my part, Spirit would meet me half way. In the dream I never saw the result. I didn't see me finding the credit card. I just saw a picture of doing the process. That was an interesting key. The dream showed me a "choice" to go look, to see if I would make the choice to and search for the credit card.

I wrote in my journal that I found the credit card. I was really happy and grateful. It was a big lesson for me. Much like a Lighthouse that stands there on land to warn and keep sailors aware of where the shore is, I think these dreams and these experiences are like my Lighthouse. They keep me aware that the Lord is very close to me and warns me. The Spiritual Warrior is receptive to the Spirit and to Spirit's guidance.

Dreams and Journal Writing

I keep a journal, a habit I acquired when I was younger, because writing things out always helps me. I write down the things that I wish, the things that have happened, and the things that I want to let go of. There's something that happens consciously when I write, either with my right hand or left hand.

Both my attunement to and remembrance of my dreams—and my journal writing—provide me with my desired outcome of being more in sync with Spirit, more receptive to Spirit, more aware of how Spirit is working with me in my life.

<u>My Method</u>: These are things that I did (and still do) on a nightly basis: When setting up for dreaming, I asked the Lord to help me and protect me. I filled a glass of water, drank a little of it, and prepared myself (sort of a ritual) before going to bed.

Before I went to sleep, I wrote a lot in my journal, asking God for answers. I wrote down, "God, please help." And that was pretty much my process of writing it all down, seeing the day and how it went by; my consciousness would show it to me like a film, and then I would write, "Oh, God, please help," or "Thank you very much," or "I'm so grateful." I was asking the Lord to help me in any way. And in the morning, I would drink that glass of water, which helped me to remember my dreams. If I woke up in the night to go to the bathroom, I wrote my dreams down immediately because when I woke up later I might forget. As much as I can remember them, I write my dreams in my journal. My dreams can be messages, they can be signs, or they can be guidance to walk the ways of the Spiritual Warrior. My inner spiritual guide is my mentor / God / J-R. What's fantastic about journal writing or keeping a diary, and I know it sounds rather corny, is that it really takes care of me. When I took the time to write, I remembered more of my dreams.

As I climbed the ranks of dreaming (like the rigging of the mastership of dreams), I prayed for inner messages, and I would get them. I saw events way before they happened. At one time I started to track maybe six months to twelve months out ahead of me, in increments. Sometimes I would dream of working as an actor. I wanted to work. I would pray, and I would have a dream that I would be with Andy Garcia or some other movie star. After seventeen years, I got to work with Andy Garcia, and from day one I had been dreaming about working with him and writing it down; finally, it manifested. I would see Benicio Del Toro or Mel Gibson at some party in the dream state. I told J-R about the dreams that I had with Tom Cruise, and two months later, J-R and I went to a movie, and Tom Cruise and Nicole Kidman were there as well. I had a conversation with him and Nicole, which was very much like my dream. I often tell my dreams to

J-R, before the dreams manifest physically, because then I can use him as proof.

If I hang in that state between being awake and falling asleep, and I don't fall asleep, if I stay in the flow with Spirit, trust and listen, I can ride the Sound Current of trembling sound, like thunder, a stream, violins, all sorts of sounds. If I pass it, I just fall asleep. This Sound Current is a spiritual state. Sometimes when I'm going into the dream state, the dream becomes part of my experience, and before I know it, I'm pulled out of my body and I remember. Sometimes it seems like seconds, at other times like hours. These experiences are priceless to me, and limitless.

As a sub-method of journaling, I found that free-form writing* has worked well for me, especially during times of pain and anger or when working through an issue that was kind of boiling inside of me. I sat down with blank paper and just wrote whatever came to me, and I wrote until it was done. Then I burned what I had written, without looking at it. I found it was best to do it right away, as the issue was happening, rather than waiting until things (and feelings) built up.

Flowing with Spirit

As an actor, I have learned a kind of Taoist way of working that can translate to the world. I know that what I chase will retreat from me. When I really want the outer goal (women/movie roles/cars), I am not going to get them. When I'm totally taking care of myself and seek God, I become detached; then along come the things I've wanted (women/movie roles/cars); they're interested in me because I'm interested in life and Spirit. It was true with the girls I chased. When I surrendered and began loving myself, then and only then would the girls come my way.

In a sense, the actor's job is to get the job, to reach for it and get it. I would play a game of pretending that I didn't want it, that I was not attached to it, which I had to eventually stop playing. Once again, I flowed with the Spirit; I let it guide me, but I was only shown little hints. And I never forget to ask for these things only if it is "For the Highest Good." I'm paraphrasing the Lord Jesus Christ here, who said, "You receive not because you ask not." I'm asking! I'm asking! But then I have to let go and allow Spirit to bring what is right for me.

Workout / Taking Care of Myself

One of my Methods is movement: exercising; running, yoga, any type of exercise that will get me out of the house. Especially when I'm feeling down or depressed, movement or exercise (not just sitting within my depression) gets me going. It moves me out of this locked vision that I'm in, which sort of paralyzes me. Not moving, not exercising, not working out becomes a Catch-22. It just keeps circling, and becomes this circle of crazies. As John-Roger has said, crazies are when a person keeps doing the same thing over and over, creating the same pattern, but expecting a different result." And the way to break "crazies" is to break the pattern.

For my Practical Treatise, one of the things I have been tracking is my weight and what that means to me. I found it means health to me. Also, at 44 years old, I really want to look good for myself. I am an actor, so there's some vanity in me that I definitely want to look "hot." I really like looking healthy for me. When my weight is up, I'm not taking care of myself. I had to have the courage to face the fat. For a while, I was stuck in the 212-pound category, and I was very depressed over not being able to hit below this mark.

Eating became a choice to avoid numbing and stuffing myself with "comfort foods." I have lost close to 55 pounds in 2007-2008. Each layer of fat or layer of pounds had, for me, a very obvious emotional, subconscious, or unconscious block. With each pound I lost, there was a feeling or a mental picture, or a flash of something in the past or present attached to it. Losing the weight unleashed a lot of things that equated to failure, such as, "I'm not good enough. I'm not worthy." A lot of it was about materiality, like my acting career. A lot of it was the focus and energy I put into the film *Spiritual Warriors*, and not enough time spent with the Spirit. At some point, I must have disengaged from making contact with Spirit and went forward into the world without sticking with the Spirit like I normally do. There are times when I *flow* in and I *flow* out. My consciousness can disconnect at times. When I *flowed* out, that's when Spirit and God and the Traveler reflected to me where I was putting my heart, my attention, and my *awareness*. I learned to come back to the Lord, to always keep my eyes on the Lord.

Taking care of myself has gone way beyond what I weigh or don't weigh. It has become staying in alignment with the Spirit.

Awareness

Spiritual Exercises help me pull back, especially when my ego is trying to run the world to the ground. When I breathe and take a moment and watch, I realize the awareness is changing. I ask the Lord / Inner Guide to help. I begin to relax, and I allow God to show me the Inner Movie of the day and how I behaved. At that moment I bring my awareness present and forgive myself for stepping out of the "flow." Making *Spiritual Warriors* forced me to look into to my methods and work them because it was easy to become attached to the film. Whatever I'm attached to in life, that becomes a test for me to see if I can remain aware, stay in the flow and be graceful.

Awareness, to me, is everything, and I'm careful about what I say or do. I'm more receptively vigilant with others. When we were shooting *Spiritual Warriors,* I found myself to be very much in that "spiritual spotlight," as I explained earlier. God had shined His Light on me, and I had the feeling that I could do no wrong. It was very similar to having been given the job of taking care of a child. I was in protective mode. It's not hard work to be in that protective state of awareness, to be slightly above the norm. I was focused on watching this kid, which is probably what God does for us. The movie *Spiritual Warriors* was like a child, and I took care of it. It required a lot of responsibility. Money was attached to it. And sometimes it didn't happen the way I wanted it to. It happened the way It/Spirit wanted it to.

Completing and Clearing with CKT

Another important area of my P.T. I chose to focus on was completion in my life and not letting projects fall into oblivion. Completing at least three things in my life each day moves me forward and brings me to my loving. These are baby steps I take on a daily basis. Keeping my house in order keeps me creative and clear with Spirit. I've experienced completing the day and then coming home to clear the day either through J-R or MH.

Over the course of the D.S.S. program, I learned a type of kinesiology testing or muscle testing called CKT. It is a method for identifying blocks in the consciousness and clearing them. I learned from John-Roger that if I identify what's bugging me, if I can name it, it can be gone. When I am able to consciously name it, check it by muscle testing, and clear it through CKT, it will often go away.

The clearing becomes easier for me because when I am completing on the physical level, I focus inside and begin clearing those things that hang on to me through procrastination. When I let the procrastinations take me over, I become paralyzed and I can start to feel the darkness set in. It's a darkness I can't explain. I ask inside for the Inner Master and the Christ to please take me out of the trap. The movement, the clearing, and completing at least three things each day gets me flowing back on the Awareness Train.

I have the luxury and the blessing of being able to work personally with John-Roger, and that has been my anchor and my *alignment* whenever I was out of balance or just off, spiritually speaking. Having the ability to choose in awareness to see J-R almost every night, that's an instant anchor point, and I thank God I was smart enough to see that. I keep choosing to realign to the Spirit, and be in the flow of the Spiritual Warrior. Ultimately, what it gets down to is this: When I get knocked down, can I get back up right away? I choose to get back up. And that's what it is; I was smart enough to do the clearing, clear myself and begin listening to when to clear. I developed the receptivity to Spirit, J-R, and God.

Outcomes

Lessons from the Making of *Spiritual Warriors*

Origins and Preparation

In 1999 John-Roger and I wrote a script together for a movie, *Spiritual Warriors*, that was inspired by his book, *Spiritual Warrior: The Art of Living Spiritually* (which became a number one *L.A. Times* Best Seller). We had collaborated on other short films, but this was our first full-length feature, and it incorporated many of the teachings that J-R has shown me. The writing of the movie was relatively fun and easy to do with the Boss. I really enjoyed collaborating with J-R, and he definitely inspired the movie and everyone involved in the shoot.

I have been a student in the D.S.S. class since 2003. The making of the movie *Spiritual Warriors* took place from 2004 to 2006. The subject of my Practical Treatise is "Living with the Spiritual Warrior." The film is a form of a Practical Treatise but presented on a DVD. I've seen a lot of miracles while working on the movie. When I watch this film, I can't help but think of the best moments of my life. I experienced God touching my head with His hand. I could do no wrong. My righteousness comes from my awareness and knowing that God loves me.

Number one, it's a film and it's entertaining.

Number two, it can profoundly change people's lives. (I've heard a few accounts of change.) It awakens people to a different way of looking at things.

Shooting this movie solidified for me that the Spiritual Warrior takes on things. It was a challenge, and it was a lesson within a lesson. There was the lesson in the life, the lessons in the Spirit, and the lessons in the movie. It was about the *flowing* with what Spirit wanted and how I learned to wait on the Spirit. I used my ego in the right moments, but I had to be aware that when I headed home at the end of the day, I needed to drop the forward ego* and touch into the Spirit—to be okay that the forward ego gets things accomplished in the world but also to be aware to come to a place of receptivity, flow, grace inside myself and others.

While I was doing all these worldly accomplishments, I think that's when the D.S.S. class became a workshop for me. It's been a workshop where I can bring in those experiences that I've had during the month, out in the world, and then I can work the workshop tools that I learned while in class. I'm able to come to a conclusion, a summation of what I've learned, what I intend to do, and what the next steps are. Sometimes I fail. I think it's very important to fail. I think it's very important to be aware that ultimately it's the same as success. It depends on my attitude. The word *failure* is not negative. Failing just means I didn't hit my mark. Success means I hit the mark.

Before I started the filming of *Spiritual Warriors,* I wanted to change my life. In 2004, I decided to "climb the mountain," so I ran the Los Angeles Marathon in March of that year. I was empowered to run the marathon in six hours. I found the strength by talking to J-R/God inwardly, being receptive to Spirit and being in the flow. I felt pain, my hands were swelling, my knees were giving up, but I kept my eye on God. I thought about the Greek man at Marathon, running to save his country. I was running to save myself. Andy Garcia had given me the role of a lifetime, the role of "Che Guevara." The running of the L.A. Marathon prepared me to make *Spiritual Warriors.* It made me strong; it made me ask inside for my Guide. It was a time and a process of trust.

Outcomes

Discovering the Inner Spiritual Warrior
Shooting, Editing, and Finishing

We shot scenes for the movie in the Middle East for nineteen days. We shot fifty-two days in the U.S., including Utah and Santa Barbara. We spent another nine months on VFX, or Visual Effects. It was done painstakingly, and it was a great film to shoot. I began learning this deep connection of intuition and inner guidance on the set of *Spiritual Warriors*. J-R gave me the courage when he gave me the reins to shoot the movie in the Middle East. It was a Light that shined on me for yet another moment in time. We were in Egypt, looking for a site to shoot the desert scenes. I was creating my own little fantasy that I was going to shoot *Lawrence of Arabia* scenes in *Spiritual Warriors*. We went further and further and further into the desert looking for the perfect shot for the film.

The director said, "Promise me it'll be no more than a half hour out here in the desert." Well, it ended up being more like an hour, and he was pissed off. We couldn't find the location that my co-producer and I wanted. The director got out of our vehicles, balled me out, and I gave in. I collapsed inside myself. So we got into the Land Rovers and proceeded back to the hotel—actually, back to the bus, which would take us on a paved highway back to the hotel about an hour and a half away. In the Land Rover heading to the bus, I was talking to others, but in my head I was talking to the Inner Master, the Inner Spiritual Warrior (a.k.a., John-Roger). I was talking in my head as if I had just arrived in Los Angeles and was talking to him physically. And it went like this:

"How was the shoot?" J-R asked. I said, "It was great. It was great, great. It was fantastic. Thank you so much, J-R." "Did you get everything you wanted?" he asked. I said, "Well, yeah, yeah, mostly, except for ... " "What is it?" he asked. I said, "Well, we didn't get, you know ... there was this shot we wanted in the desert, and the director said I broke the agreement, so I didn't get the shot. And it could have been just beautiful, just like in *Lawrence of Arabia*. "So you didn't get the shot?" he asked. "No ... ," I said with regret. "So you just collapsed and went ahead and did what the director wanted to do?" he said. "Yeah, that's it," I said crying. I was even more depressed.

At that point, I yelled in the walkie-talkies, "Stop! "Stop the cars!" I shouted, "Stop!" We all stopped. All the Land Rovers huddled in the desert, surrounded by sand dunes. The director and the cinematographer stepped out of their cars. There was a mutiny in the middle of the desert. And basically, all hell came out of my mouth, and I said, "If you don't get the camera out and film me walking across the sand dunes (my *Intuition flow*), I will fire all of you." Half the people were on my side, the other half on their side. The cinematographer gave up and said, "Peace, peace, peace. Let's shoot this." We shot the "Dune Scene" as the sun was setting, and it was reflecting off the sand. I was wearing my galabeya (a traditional Egyptian garment), crossing the desert (just like Peter O'Toole in *Lawrence of Arabia*, where he stands on the sand dune with the wind blowing at his white galabeya, and he stares at his knife reflecting his image). During our dailies, the director apologized and said, "That was a great shot." I explained to him what had happened in my head, speaking to John-Roger, my Inner Master. He said, "Jeez, I wish you would've told me that at the time it was happening. All I heard was, *Get the hell out of the car!*"

Listening and Being Receptive to Spirit

In order to complete filming, we were doing some reshooting at the Standard Studios. The use of a studio allowed us to do "green screen" work (CGI, or Computer Generated Images).

John-Roger was there supporting me that day. In the script there was a scene in which I was holding an infant. The infant represents the Soul visually, and I was supposed to be reconciling things with this infant, a Christ-like figure or a Basic Self. In this scene the objective was to have love emanating from the screen, so that the audience would experience blissfulness. We found the infant, and the baby seemed to be okay. We shot the scene. Then the baby had to go home with the parent very soon after the shoot.

We found out later that the camera was broken. The camera had not recorded the baby. So two hours working with this baby was wasted and gone. We were in a pickle. We immediately found another baby and had the mother bring the child ASAP to us. The second baby did not want to have anything to do with me. It was crying, like babies do. It was a disaster.

I basically knelt down to J-R and said, "Please help. This is crazy." And out of J-R's mouth came, "Spirit doesn't want to do what you want to do; It wants to do what It wants to do. So find out what It wants to do." And I was stunned! I said, "Well, what does It want to do? What does It want me to do? I'll do it. I'll do it. I'll do it."

I had previously invited my friend MH and his son Danny to the set. So here they were. Daniel just turned five or so at the time; it was his birthday. He's a very loving kid. He came and ran into my arms and hugged me he was just flying high. I think I remember J-R saying, "Why don't you use Danny?" And I was thinking, "No, I need an infant." But when he hugged me, I realized, "Oh, my God, this is the kid! This child is displaying love, and I get it." I felt good when he hugged me. The director saw it and said, "Can you do it again? We'll give you a Birthday Gift." We were basically giving him his birthday gift right there and then: a role in *Spiritual Warriors*.

He did every take perfectly. What I learned from that lesson, basically, was to do what Spirit wants, not what I want. And it doesn't mean giving up my life or anything like that. It was that the guidance of the Spirit was way more important and more *flowing*, and it was way better than I had hoped.

The Spiritual Warrior had come alive in me. I listened inwardly. I checked my awareness. I made the right choice, not from ego but from a sense of what was needed to be in flow, in the Zone, true to Spirit's vision of this movie. I did what Spirit wanted, not what I wanted. The application could have been smoother on my part.

The Movie: Completion and Distribution

As of this writing, *Spiritual Warriors* has screened around the world in 33 cities in 11 countries and over 16,000 people have seen *Spiritual Warriors*. It continues to amaze me. In Israel in 2007, J-R told me the Christ energy would bless this film. I've seen with my own eyes the magic that the blessings have produced: sold-out screenings and people sharing about how the movie has profoundly changed their lives. All the different countries where we have shown the film prove to me that we are all connected. The film's context has flow, receptivity to Spirit, Love, Grace, and surrendering to the Spirit. For me, this film is an anchor in my life, to take a moment and become aware, to make the right choices and therefore receive positive results.

Spiritual Warriors has done very well, screening worldwide. Again, as I said earlier in the P.T., Spirit does not want to do what you want it to do, rather it wants to do what it wants to do, and it is doing what it wants to do. I pray every day that I hear the signs of Spirit and that I follow what it wants to do. Things are unfolding. I just have to keep reminding myself not to limit my consciousness and my ideas to this fantastical, limitless experience. It's boundless, and priceless. It comes from up above, from God, and it showers down to us.

Outcomes

For one shining moment ... there was Camelot

While shooting *Spiritual Warriors*, there were moments where I was *aligned, in sync*. I had this amazing experience of God shining the Light on me again, and there I was; wherever I went, it shined the Light on me. Of course, I checked inside, so I wouldn't "go rogue" with the energy. I knew if I misused or abused the energy, I would pay for it. It would disengage. It's just a great feeling when I know I am doing everything right. And I am. My decisions are just "Rock-n-Roll," because I'm *trusting*, in *alignment* and in the *flow* of God's will.

I seek everything in loving and in the name of God, Christ, J-R; I seek to be *aligned* to that, to *flow* in that. When I'm *aligned* to Spirit I feel the love, and I feel the spiritual awareness; and then I silently listen to what people are saying. When I'm really listening to what people are saying to me, I find they may be saying something else. I start to see what their problem is and that it isn't personal.

Selling *Spiritual Warriors*

In United Kingdom, Great Britain, we had two wonderful screenings of *Spiritual Warriors*, and both of them were pretty sold-out. John-Roger was there with friends, along with John Morton, and quite a number of the community at large came by to see it as well as a lot of newcomers. Probably eighty to ninety percent of the audiences were new people, not affiliated with MSIA; but they had heard about it through a friend, or received one of our many emails which went out, or they heard by word-of-mouth or postcards.

The South American Tour began with MA and AP working diligently to get us accepted to the Cartagena Film Festival, located on the Caribbean coast of Colombia. Once it was accepted,

MA and ZG spearheaded the project for a year. Before we knew it over 150 South Americans in MSIA arrived in Cartagena for the Festival, along with over forty Americans from MSIA. It was a party! With the help of NOW Productions and VER, PD and I went ahead to Cartagena to set up the video equipment; we wanted to have a great opening at the "Teatro Heredia," which seats 600 people. The Theatre was named after the Spanish Conquistador Don Pedro de Heredia, founder of Cartagena. The name Cartagena is the Spanish name for a base for the Carthaginians in Spain during the Roman era. (Note: I forced myself to perfect my Spanish, so that I could begin to understand Portuguese. Thanks for the schooling, J-R!)

We prepared for J-R and about twenty-five others to arrive in Cartagena. We met them at the airport and bused them to the famous El Caribe Hotel. I had been there once on a film location twenty years before, and it is a beautiful, pink, colonial-style hotel. Dating back to the 1940s, this hotel is very similar in looks to one in Havana, Cuba, the Hotel National. J-R and I had stayed there once for a film festival for our film, *My Little Havana.*

Our travel agent, BD, did a great job booking flights and hotels and getting everyone their rooms. One thing I learned is what you plan for on paper will most definitely not be reality. We had MA, CL, and many more, "Colombian Light Angels," helping to lead the many friends and families that would fill the lobby of the hotel every night for the different events.

I was happy to see my mother when she came to Cartagena. I had prayed to God when I was younger, during bad times, to please take care of my mother. Well, my mother is in great hands: God's Hands.

The (inner) trumpets blasted a sound across the lands of South America that J-R had landed in Colombia, the New Granada. John Morton, of course, brought his presence, and his support was awesome in how he held for J-R and the film. JM also held

Outcomes

a packed house for a Question & Answer Seminar. The Q&A started small, but when the assembled participants heard the news that "The Travelers" had arrived, the people began to multiply. This was a sight to behold.

My old PAT IV buddy from 1988, John Marin, showed up and it was like old times. During a Q&A someone asked me, "What is Spirit?" I said, "For me, Spirit and love mean traveling to foreign places with J-R and our family and friends in fellowship with each other." We threw a welcoming dinner party at MA for J-R and friends. That was a magical night. We all shared in a great soup called "Ajiaco." Ingredients are three varieties of potatoes, the herb Galinsoga parviflora, known locally as *guascas,* corn, and chicken. It can be garnished with capers, avocado slices, pieces of corn on the cob, and sour cream. Tasty!

We met family and friends from The Cartagena Film Festival, including The Honorable Victor Nieto, founder and leader of the Festival for forty-eight years. GN, son of VN, and his family were our guides and trusted friends. We also met up with SB and MP. We needed a leader and a Consignor to direct and assimilate information, and the Great Amelia stepped forward beautifully. I love her. She was on point.

For a grand gesture, we hired horse carriages to take us to the "Teatro Heredia," and then back to the El Caribe Hotel afterward. That had a romance that I can't explain. Imagine a twenty-horse carriage procession trotting towards "Teatro Heredia" for the premiere of *Spiritual Warriors*. One of the highlights for me was standing on stage at the "Teatro Heredia," and looking at over 600 people ready to watch *Spiritual Warriors*. J-R was in the audience and that's all I needed.

More Highlights: • Screening *Spiritual Warriors* for the second time, in the open-air Plaza de la Aduana under the stars. J-R attended, along with a packed house. We had over 400 people that night. • Dinners with an average of 30 people at colonial-style restaurants much like "El Floridita" in Havana, Cuba. • Speaking at the University of Buenaventura. John Morton and I spoke to the students there about life, Spirit, and movies; when we finished, they all flocked around J-R to get free signed copies of his *Spiritual Warrior* book. • The last day was an excursion out to the Island of Baru. A family-size group of sixty-seven people just relaxed in the Caribbean sun. It was very special. And then J-R and the Magical Circus crowds left town, and I continued on the South American Tour.

*Allow the Spirit to become manifest,
but not in terms of your anxieties,
your irritabilities,
or your consciousness of time.
Spiritual Warriors step outside of time and
await the Spirit in patience.*

– John-Roger
From: Spiritual Warrior,
The Art of Spiritual Living
(Source: www.lovingeachday.org)

*The Spiritual Warrior looks at death and loves death.
Death comes not as one who obliterates, but as one
who releases from pain and sorrow.*

– John-Roger, D.S.S.
From: Spiritual Warrior:
The Art of Spiritual Living

Being Patient with Myself

An Unexpected Outcome
of My Practical Treatise

It's now 2008, and it's become a very challenging approach at this point. There was the writing of *Spiritual Warriors* with J-R; there was the editing of the film; there was the finishing of the film; and now there is the selling of the film. It's 2008 and I don't know. I've learned to take the back seat and let the Spirit lead. It's a trusting process.

I must say that one of the things I've learned, which is applicable to my D.S.S. process and my P.T., is that it really isn't over. And that goes to my experience with my computer hard drives. While writing the first daft of this P.T., all of a sudden my external hard drives failed, which had thousands of dollars of media backed-up in them. On the exterior they were broken, the shell of the hard drive was not spinning, was not turning on. But I opened them up, and the hard drives were alive, so we began recovering the data. As they say, it's not over until the hard drive stops spinning—an analogy but still true.

In that experience, I remember John-Roger telling me, "Why don't you send it to NOW Productions? Why don't you get a second look at it?" And I was very judgmental in saying, "Oh, no, they don't know anything." In fact, they knew more than I did. That sort of set me clear that others know more than I do. Once again I was not *in sync* with Spirit. I let my ego resist and I stopped listening. Being upset or angry at what I can't control is an ego position. That position is just me wanting to do what I want to do. But what I really want to be able to do is what Spirit wants me to do and not what I want to do: to stay *in sync* with Spirit.

One of the things I heard from John-Roger the night the hard drive broke was, "Be patient with your self." What I realized is that by being patient with myself, Spirit brings my life more flow, Grace, awareness, and love because there's no fighting. Patience is very hard for me to accept; however, Spirit brings these experiences that force me to reflect on my choices and awareness. With patience comes the flow and grace and most of all the receptivity to be available for the Spirit's guidance.

I believe that the *Spiritual Warriors* film is in its own Spirit timing. It has its own patience, and I just have to *align* myself to Spirit and cooperate with what it wants to do, not what I want to do. Even if I want to get millions of dollars right away, and I want to become a Super Star, "Be Patient" is what I hear inside. I believe that was one of my biggest challenges and also one of the most awesome experiences I have had during the entire year of 2006 and most of 2007.

Being Patient with Myself

Living with a Spiritual Warrior and *Spiritual Warriors*, the Film

Since the very beginning, when I started D.S.S., I began the quest to make this movie with John-Roger, *Spiritual Warriors*. There were several processes that I became involved in. One of them was the writing of the movie, which was relatively fun and easy to do with the Boss. I will give you a parallel analogy. It's kind of like hiring a contractor and starting to build a house. Some of the contractors are bad. Some of them don't know what they're doing, and some of them don't know the job that you hired them to do. But some of them do, and so the house gets built.

Once the movie was filmed, edited, and completed, the last part was getting people into the seats to watch it and, with that, selling the movie. I'm now at the juncture of selling the movie. That has played a huge role in terms of what I've been learning throughout 2006 and 2007. The film was finished in May or June of 2006. Since then, *Spiritual Warriors* has screened around the world in 33 cities in 11 countries and over 16,000 people have seen the film. We've traveled as far as Israel and the United Kingdom; Cairo, Egypt; South America; and there are many more places to go. Things are really building up as I finish this P.T.

Also, if I think it's over, I have to remember not to believe it. I have to ask for help. I go inside and pray, listen, and stay aware. To flow and become aware and receptive to Spirit is the way of the Spiritual Warrior; that's what the Spiritual experience means inside of me.

After many years of trying to get famous and be in a film where I'm the star and all that worldly stuff, I realized it's perfect and I wouldn't want to change a thing. To be able to serve, and to see with my own eyes what the film *Spiritual Warriors* is doing out there, just plain shocks me every time. There is no logical way to explain the experiences that people are having. I'm very grateful that the film was and is the catalyst for the activities that the film has inspired around the world.

Even when confronted with adversity, the classic warrior holds fast to his values and principles. But while most warriors march off to subdue a perceived enemy, Spiritual Warriors follow a different path, marching into their own innermost center. They strive to perfect the internal discipline that will keep them attuned to God (or spirit, if you prefer that term) as they journey through this world.

– JOHN-ROGER, D.S.S.

*The Spiritual Warrior accepts all things.
This means no judgment and no resistance.
(No one ever said that these practices were easy!)*

– JOHN-ROGER, D.S.S.

Ten-Week Repeatability Study with Others

घु

Another requirement of the D.S.S. program, in addition to writing a Practical Treatise, is to create a sixty-six-day Repeatability Study. I started with ten participants and finished with nine. Three of the participants were from MSIA; the other six participants I found on "My Space," an online Internet social forum where people meet and create friendships without ever physically meeting.

I asked each participant to complete a "pre-study" Questionnaire and "Study Disclaimer Agreement" and had them return them to me by fax or send them by email. I also put a video of instructions on "YouTube," which is an online television forum that allows anyone to upload any video. The Repeatability Study package I sent them included an Excel file with the tracking information, the Repeatability Study directions, the pre- and post-study Questionnaires, and the web links to "Youtube.com."

1. <u>Methods</u>: I asked the participants in the Study to consistently do five specific practices daily, following the methods that had worked for me. My hypothesis was that IF they did these activities regularly, THEN they would experience more of the qualities of the Spiritual Warrior, specifically "Love." What was true Love for them? Loving unconditionally.
2. Confidently making choices. A Hero. A Leader. To be clear in their choices.
3. Focusing their internal attention, even when the external realities of their everyday life were chaotic, troublesome, or just plain annoying. Focusing on their Inner guide.
4. Knowing the Inner and Outer worlds in awareness.
5. The courage to see themselves, God, and Truth.
6. Greater Family / Fellowship.

1) Exercise / Movement / Light Body
2) Completing at least three things each day
3) S.E.'s / Meditation, ten minutes each day
4) Dialogue with Inner Master
5) Writing in a Journal for Dreams or Spiritual Wisdom

<u>Results</u>:
The Pre- and Post-Study questionnaires were the same. Each question could be answered by circling a word that best described the participant's experience. The five questions were: I Experience?

1) My physical health: (Excellent, Good, Not so good, Pretty Bad)

Ten-Week Repeatability Study with Others

2) More Grace in my life: (Often, Sometimes, Hardly Ever, Never)

3) Receptive to Spiritual Wisdom: (Often, Sometimes, Hardly Ever, Never)

4) Inner Master Reveals, "Did I hold strong?" or "Did I collapse?" (Often, Sometimes, Hardly Ever, Never)

5) Dreams remembered, receiving messages of wisdom: (Often, Sometimes, Hardly Ever, Never)

I asked the nine participants to track their experiences for ten weeks, to record their progress daily, and then measure their results in the bottom five categories. At the end of the study, they completed the "post-study" Questionnaire. I Experience?

6) My physical health: (Excellent, Good, Not so good, Pretty Bad)

7) More Grace in my life: (Often, Sometimes, Hardly Ever, Never)

8) Receptive to Spiritual Wisdom: (Often, Sometimes, Hardly Ever, Never)

9) Inner Master Reveals, "Did I hold strong" or "Did I collapse?" (Often, Sometimes, Hardly Ever, Never)

10) Dreams remembered, receiving messages of wisdom: (Often, Sometimes, Hardly Ever, Never)

The participants were assigned numbers to protect their identities. Participants 1 through 3 are MSIA students, numbers 4 through 9 were not. My total participants were 9.

Everyone experienced some positive change as a result of this study, as shown in the chart of their Pre- and Post-Study Questionnaire responses.

These were the best study participants that expressed their experiences. They didn't stop or give up, and I am grateful to them. The three people involved in MSIA found a deeper connection, and they all three rededicated themselves to the spiritual work and J-R. The other six participants found their results from the Repeatability Study to be meaningful, and it was reflected to them in their daily life, which they normally didn't pay any attention to. It's clear in looking at their tracking sheets that by participating in this Study they found the traits of Spiritual Warrior:

1. "Love." Loving unconditionally.
2. Confidently making choices. A Hero. A Leader.
3. Focusing their internal attention, even when the external realities of their everyday life were chaotic, troublesome, or just plain annoying. Focusing on their Inner guide.
4. Knowing their Inner and Outer worlds in awareness.
5. The courage to see God and their Truth.
6. Family / Fellowship.

The best feedback I received is from the participants' letters/emails and quotes.

Ten-Week Repeatability Study with Others

Example:

#2. "Thanks so much for letting me participate in this study. Since I started the study I have increased greatly my checking inside with my Inner Master / J-R; I have heard stronger guidance that seems to have been very accurate and effective for me. Perhaps the biggest impact has been in my holding strong with what is true for me, particularly with strong personalities in my life. I intend to keep using the tools of tracking what wisdoms I'm getting and of checking in with J-R inwardly because these have been very helpful. LL, 2."

#4. "The truth is that the program has really done a lot to help me with staying focused on completing at least three things a day, even when I didn't feel like it, dreaming deeper and paying attention to those dreams, every detail, and what they reveal, and in becoming far more spiritual in my meditation and prayers. It's also helped me to rely more on myself (with the 'Inner Master') and I do feel more grace in my life each day because of these daily practices. It's also helped me to be a more forgiving person who tries to understand human flaws on a more personal level. I do feel that I've grown in ways that I wouldn't have expected to when I first started. Sincerely, #4."

#4. 7/31/07: "I woke up this morning feeling happy. I woke still singing that song over and over again in my mind from The Sound of Music, 'I am sixteen going on seventeen . . . I will be there for you.' It was that innocent kind of happiness where you have all these thoughts about your future and life seems so hopeful. Maybe I saw this program as a kind of fresh start for getting refocused, and maybe that's why I dreamed that and woke up happy."

#4. *8/3/07:* "*Personal Reflection: Yesterday in the* Loving Each Day *email, I thought about what it said about hindsight and activating 'hindsight'—looking down the road and seeing how you will feel 'afterward' about something before you do it. I thought about so many decisions I've regretted with the words, 'If only . . .' So I saved that message. Just the day before that, I'd also read something similar in the book,* Journey of a Soul, *about your <u>conscious</u> self and how we so often say, act, feel, and do things from this state of mind and state of living.*"

#5. "*I started on the 6th. The most I'd say that has more effect on me is the meditation. The sensations of energy are intense; it's consistent so I'm used to it, but it's a good thing. I've always surrounded myself everyday with the white light of the Holy Spirit; it's normal for me.*"

#1. "*Notes on the week: My dreams are starting to be remembered in great detail, which I am journaling. This is after many, many years of not remembering. Also, I like the talking to the Inner Master. For me J-R, my traveler. I've noticed an increase in awareness, guidance, and the Sound Current. I added weighing myself one time a week as I'm working on releasing weight. I like the 3 completions, as I'm driven more to complete in my personal life. I complete a lot with my work and service, and am now spending more time on completions in my personal life. Thanks. I'm into the work.*"

#9. "*Thanks for bringing this into my life.*"

#8. "*I'm done with my tracking sheets and I've read many sections of* Spiritual Warrior *over and over, and I washed dishes to reflect on my day. Although I probably won't be continuing the tracking sheets, I will certainly continue to read books by*

Ten-Week Repeatability Study with Others

Dr. John-Roger, listen to his CDs and study other material associated with MSIA. I'll still do the Light Body and S.E.'s."

I watched the process and it was amazing because I stood back and waited. I trusted. I looked away to something else, and by the time the participants finished, I turned to look and it was a beautiful sight. I felt very detached from the participants and their outcomes. I let the Spirit work and stayed out of Spirit's way. This process was one of listening to my Inner guide, allowing the awareness to show to me the positive choices that will lead to greater results.

*Spiritual Warriors are open to the world,
not shut off from it.
They do not ask to control it
but accept it as it is and seek inner guidance
in order to respond to it in ways
that are aligned with their highest intentions.
They know that the fears,
aggravations, and confusions of life
aren't accidental;
instead, our Souls can take advantage of
the particular opportunities they offer—
opportunities to learn, grow, and share.*

– JOHN-ROGER
FROM: SPIRITUAL WARRIOR,
THE ART OF SPIRITUAL LIVING
(SOURCE: WWW.LOVINGEACHDAY.ORG)

Conclusions

ह्रू

Initiations in the Nile of Love

How do I live with my Spiritual Warrior? I live with it very carefully and very easily with awareness. For example, I used to struggle to fall asleep while everyone else in the house was asleep. The world was asleep. It might have been 2:00 or 3:00 in the morning, but I was not asleep. Sometimes I felt that I was in a higher state. Sometimes I was just aware of hearing things in my mind. I think J-R has mentioned that it's sometimes like a radio station with many channels, and you can hear every radio station that there is out there and every noise: the crying, the laughing, the sighing, the agony, and the horror. There is this cacophony of music that the universe is composing. I have experienced that, and it's very strange. Sometimes I can also hear the whooshing (like the sound of a seashell when held against your ear) when it's completely silent in the room. I wonder, "Are these things spiritual? Are they real? Are they not?" I know there are other worlds beyond this one. Being a Spiritual Warrior entails being aware, listening to whatever we attune to, being receptive to Spirit.

I think the key thing of spiritual work and the P.T., working in the spiritual world and life, is to continue to make myself available to it. Because once I numb it, it's so hard to awaken what took me eons to awaken. Sometimes I put it to sleep because I can't handle it. It's definitely work to awaken, to get up, to be aware. Ever since I started the Master's class and the P.T., it's been a life-changing situation for me. Making the movie *Spiritual Warriors* has paralleled that, and it has paralleled the lessons that I have learned.

John-Roger, the ultimate Spiritual Warrior, is definitely my anchor point to remind me of all the lessons of the Spiritual Warrior within me. And that's one thing about J-R; he's always holding the loving. He's always able to balance himself and balance everyone else with him. It is wonderful to have a master, a Wayshower, here on Earth, and J-R definitely demonstrates it. He is a real Spiritual Warrior. He embodies all the things I have continued to learn and want to become. I want him to be my Teacher and my Master always.

*The Spiritual Warrior cooperates with all things.
You know you are not in control,
but it looks as if you are.*

– JOHN-ROGER, D.S.S.

*The Spiritual Warrior understands all things.
This doesn't mean you can explain everything
that is going on within you; you just have
to awaken to your experience of it.
Then understanding appears.*

– JOHN-ROGER, D.S.S.

Epilogue

घु

What I'm about to share is the result of being receptive to Spirit / God, especially when I'm in the flow, grace and listening and watching the ego.

In reflecting on the Rock-Star Tour of *Spiritual Warriors* through South America, I thought a lot about Christopher Columbus, or as they call him there, "Cristobal Colón." I discovered, through the Light / J-R that guided me (which was already there), an audience filled with hunger for the Spirit and for the love of the Traveler. This energy that runs through MSIA (as well as the several other Traveler organizations*) is so very present in South America. Some people have heard of the Traveler* or Dr. John-Roger only via video or on audio tapes, the Soul Awareness Discourses or Home Seminars. Maybe their local reps have talked to them about J-R, but many have never met J-R. There are so many people that I met on this tour who have never met J-R physically; yet they know him on the Inner. I found them to be stronger in the Inner because there is no outer form to rely on, no excuse of "Oh, I'll see J-R at Conference or

Easter or Christmas." I had to ask myself, "How strong am I on the inside?"

(Flashback to the ancient times when the leader would speak to the tribe of their hero's feats.) J-R is now a living legend in many of these parts. I was having dinner with an MSIA minister in South America, and they were telling me how great J-R is; it felt like they had hung out with J-R before. So I asked, "When was it you met J-R?" They replied, "Never." I realized at that moment how lucky and blessed I am. This tugs at my emotions and makes me appreciate J-R even more.

Love you, J-R.

Baruch Bashan

*The Spiritual Warrior has enthusiasm for all things.
When you open to the Spirit, Its energy
pours through you, and you regain
the wonder and awe of life.*

– JOHN-ROGER, D.S.S.

*The Spiritual Warrior has empathy for all things.
Others are going through the same trials as you,
so there is no need to feel superior or inferior.*

– JOHN-ROGER, D.S.S.

APPENDIX I
Ordination Blessing

घू

Ministerial Ordination

Ordination is done through the line of the Melchizedek Priesthood, which is a true, unbroken line, straight into Christ, straight into God. Melchizedek was the first priest who was blessed by God, and that line comes through Abraham to Christ and to us, the ministers. My Blessing from my ministerial ordination (see below) is a big key to my Practical Treatise. In the Movement of Spiritual Inner Awareness (MSIA), after two years of studying Soul Awareness Discourses, a person can apply to become a minister in MSIA. What I love about doing my ministry is that I don't have to convert anybody. Being a minister in the Movement of Spiritual Inner Awareness is about being of service, in an ordinary way. Half the time I'm not conscious that I'm a minister. I just go on with my life, placing Light where it needs to be. I don't have to wear special clothing to do that. I don't need permission to minister to anyone or anything. Jesus said, something to the effect of, "You, too, shall do what I do, and even greater." If two or more are gathered in the name of the Christ, and in the name of God, that's a ministry. The guidelines are simple: Don't hurt yourself, don't hurt others; take care of yourself, so you can help take care of others; and use everything for upliftment, learning, and growth. Becoming a minister changed my life, and I really do love my ministry. My ministry is to take care of the boss, John-Roger, and do what I can to promote *Spiritual Warriors*, the film. I was blown away in 2007, when I received the MSIA Minister of the Year award. Winning the Minister of the Year award was a great fantasy fulfillment for me. I transformed it into winning an Oscar or a Golden Globe award. If I never win other awards, I can rest assured that I got the experience of winning.

Ordination Blessing
August 29, 1988

JM: "Today is Monday, August 29, 1988. This is an ordination on—and we're going to have you say your own name out loud.
JG: "Jesus Garcia."
JM: "And the ministers present are: … "AG," "AP," "MD," "PD", "TS"
JM: "And John Morton."
[Preamble:] "Father, we ask for the clearing. Jesus Garcia, we, as Ministers of God and of love and light and sound stand by you at this time, placing our hands upon your head, conferring upon you the Ordination of Minister in the Movement

Ordination Blessing

of Spiritual Inner Awareness. We do this through the order of the Melchizedek Priesthood, the office of Christ, the Mystical Traveler and Preceptor Consciousnesses, and into God. This delineates for you the divine line of authority by which we call forward God's Light to do work in this world. We say to you then, go forward into the world, ministering to all, regardless of race, creed, color, situation, circumstance, or environment. And at this time Spirit brings the Blessing:

"This blessing is a delicious presence, something that you can feel in all of your being, through all of your body, through all of your cells, through every part of who you are. And begin this blessing each moment that you breathe in, that you renew your life, that you are purifying your consciousness, to stand into the heritage that is this line of the Traveler, to step forward and honor the true self, beginning to open your consciousness now. As you allow yourself to step forward and you honor the integrity of your being, words of wisdom can come forth, and you speak the words of truth. Let your words be ones that are of a loving nature, that are the essence of this being that is of the Traveler. Bring your discipline from the heart. Let it be a loving waltz with God that you dance and sing the heritage of your being. No man is a fool, who lets himself sing and praise the Lord. There is a great privilege in this Ministry, and it comes through your own honoring, your own willingness to step forward. So begin in this moment and lift your head, for you are now in high ground from this day forward. We stand by you, we love you, we support you, and we bless you. Baruch Bashan."
Congregation: "Baruch Bashan."

A comment on the ministerial blessing: It was August 1988 when I was ordained near London, England. Other ministers, and many of my family and friends from MSIA, were there that day; those people helped shape my life, and they continue to support me and hold the Light for my life and Soul. J-R was also there, observing as the Ordination took place. The Ordination, to me, was packed with energy and power, spiritual energy that can't really be analyzed.

A key phrase in the Blessing for me was, "No man is a fool who sings and praises the Lord." I take that to mean I love to sing and I love also to praise the Lord. Singing has always brought me to a mellow place. I love to sing and play guitar. Presently, I'm writing music, working on my double album, and it's been very healing. Another key phrase was, "Let it be a loving waltz with God that you dance and sing the heritage of your being." My experience has been I've always loved to sing and dance, those things bring joy to me. When I have joy and enthusiasm in my life, I feel closer to God. And I know in my heart that it works.

*When you feel really negative and you talk
about it—not as a victim but as a way of facing
the enemy and loving it—you are saying,
"Out of God come all things." All things.
That includes the negative things, too.
Negative doesn't mean bad;
we make things bad by judging them.*

– JOHN-ROGER, D.S.S.

*Be in this world as if you were a stranger
or a traveler along a path.*

– Mohammed

APPENDIX II

Glossary

हु

Akashic Records. The vast spiritual records in which every Soul's entire experiences are recorded.

Ani-Hu. A chant used in MSIA. HU is Sanskrit and is an ancient name for God, and ANI adds the quality of empathy.

Ascended Masters. Non-physical beings of high spiritual development that are part of the spiritual hierarchy. May work out of any realm above the **physical realm.** *See also Spiritual Hierarchy.*

Astral Realm. The psychic, material realm above the physical realm. The realm of the imagination. Intertwines with the physical as a vibratory rate.

Astral Travel. Occurs when the consciousness leaves the physical body to travel in the astral realm.

Aura. The electro-magnetic energy field that surrounds the human body. Has color and movement.

Baruch Bashan (bay-roosh bay-shān). Hebrew words meaning "The blessings already are." The blessings of Spirit exist in the here and now.

Basic Self. Has responsibility for bodily functions; maintains habits and the psychic centers of the physical body. Also known as the lower self. Handles prayers from the physical to the High Self. *See also Conscious Self and High Self.*

Beloved. The Soul; the God within.

Causal Realm. The psychic, material realm above the astral realm and below the mental realm. Intertwines somewhat with the physical realm as a vibratory rate.

Chakra. A psychic center of the body.

Christ Consciousness. A universal consciousness of pure Spirit. Exists within each person through the Soul.

Christ, office of the. The Christ is a spiritual office, much like the presidency of the United States. Many people have filled that office; Jesus the Christ filled it more fully than any other being. One of the highest offices in the realms of Light.

Chumash Indians. The Chumash are a Native American people who historically inhabit mainly the southern coastal regions of California, in the vicinity of what is now San Luis Obispo, Santa Barbara, Ventura, and Los Angeles counties, extending from Morro Bay in the north to Malibu in the south. They also occupied three of the Channel Islands: Santa Cruz, Santa Rosa, and San Miguel; the smaller island of Anacapa was uninhabited. Modern place names with Chumash origins include Malibu, Lompoc, Ojai, Point Mugu, Piru, Lake Castaic, and Simi Valley.

Conscious Self. The self that makes conscious choices. It is the "captain of the ship," in that it can override both the Basic Self and the High Self. The self that comes in as a "tabula rasa," or "blank slate." See also Basic Self and High Self.

Cosmic Mirror. The mirror at the top of the void, which is at the top of the etheric realm, just below the Soul realm. Everything that has not been cleared in the physical, astral, causal, and mental levels is projected onto the cosmic mirror.

Crown Chakra. The psychic center at the top of the head.

Devas. Non-physical beings from the Devic Kingdom that serve humankind by caring for the elements of nature. They support the proper functioning of all natural things on the planet.

Discourses. *See Soul Awareness Discourses.*

Dream Master. A spiritual master with whom the Mystical Traveler works, and who assists one in balancing past actions while dreaming.

Etheric Realm. The psychic, material realm above the mental realm and below **the Soul Realm**. Equated with the unconscious or subconscious level. Sometimes known as the Esoteric Realm.

False Self. Can be thought of as the ego, the individualized personality that incorrectly perceives itself to be fundamentally separated from others and God.

Free-Form Writing. This is John-Roger's technique on how to free negative thoughts through writing them out. (See p. 23 in *Spiritual Warrior: The Art of Living*.)

Forward-Ego. When the ego is involved with the outer world rather than within one's own inner self.

Galabeya. A tunic worn by Egyptian men and women. The galabeya is the traditional garment of Egypt and is often worn with a Lasa, a silk scarf worn around the shoulders. The galabeya is similar to the abaya, a more decorative tunic that would be worn for more formal or festive occasions. The tunya is a garment, similar to the galabeya, worn by monks, priests, and bishops of the Coptic Church during liturgy prayers. The tunya is worn by clergy members over the galabeya.

Grace. Grace has feelings of joy, laughter, and forgiveness that transcend the current Karma. Jesus Christ is Grace and has extended his love to us.

Great White Brotherhood. Non-physical spiritual beings working in service to mankind in the spiritual line of the Christ and Mystical Traveler. They can assist with spiritual clearing and upliftment.

Guide Inner. *(see Inner Master)*

High Self. The self that functions as one's spiritual guardian, directing the Conscious Self towards those experiences that are for one's greatest **spiritual progression**. Has knowledge of the destiny pattern agreed upon **before embodiment.** *See also Basic Self, Conscious Self, and Karmic Board.*

Glossary

Holy Spirit. The positive energy of Light and Sound that comes from the supreme God. The life force that sustains everything in all creation. Often uses the magnetic Light through which to work on the psychic, material realms. Works only for the highest good. Is the third part of the Trinity or Godhead.

Hu. A "tone," or sound, that is an ancient name of the supreme God.

Initiation. In MSIA, the process of being connected to the Sound Current of God.

Initiation Tone. In MSIA, spiritually charged words given to an initiate in a Sound Current initiation. The name of the Lord of the realm into which the person is being initiated.

Inner Levels / Realms. The astral, causal, mental, etheric, and Soul realms that exist within a person's consciousness. *See also Outer Levels / Realms.*

Inner Master. The inner expression of the Mystical Traveler, existing within a person's consciousness.

Insight Seminars. John-Roger founded this Organization. A five-day course that focuses on awakening of the heart.

Kal Power / Kal Niranjan. The power of the Lord of all the negative realms. Has authority over the physical realm. Functions out of the causal realm.

Karma. The law of cause and effect: as you sow, so shall you reap. The responsibility of each person for his or her actions. The law that directs and sometimes dominates a being's physical existence.

Karmic Board. A group of non-physical spiritual masters who meet with a being before embodiment to assist in the planning of that being's spiritual journey on Earth. The Mystical Traveler has a function in this group.

Light, Spiritual. The energy of Spirit that pervades all realms of existence. Also refers to the Light of the Holy Spirit.

Light, Magnetic. The Light of God that functions in the psychic, material realms. Not as high as the Light of the Holy Spirit, and does not necessarily function for the highest good. *See also Light and Holy Spirit.*

Light Masters. Non-physical spiritual teachers who work on the psychic, material realms to assist people in their spiritual progression.

Line of the Travelers. The line of spiritual energy extending from the Mystical Traveler Consciousness, in which the Mystical Traveler's students function.

Lord of Realm. Each realm (physical, astral, causal, mental, etheric, and Soul) has a Lord that directs that realm. The Lord of a realm is subservient to the Lords of the realms above it. All of the Lords of the psychic, material realms are subservient to the Lord of all negative creation, which manifests as the Kal Power. The Lord of the Soul realm has authority over all Lords of realms below the Soul realm, including the Kal Power. *See also Kal Power.*

Lords of Karma. *See Karmic Board.*

Masters of Light. *See Light Masters.*

Glossary

Melchizedek Priesthood. Melchizedek was the first priest who was blessed by God; those ordained in this priesthood are part of a true line, straight into Christ, straight into God, and through that to Christ, to us, the ministers.

Mental Realm. The psychic, material realm above the causal realm and below the etheric realm. Relates to the universal mind. The source of the individual mind.

Movement of Spiritual Inner Awareness (MSIA). An organization whose major focus is to bring people into an awareness of Soul Transcendence. John-Roger is the founder. Mystery Schools. Schools in Spirit, in which initiates receive training and instruction. Initiates of the Traveler Consciousness study in mystery schools that are under the Traveler's auspices.

Mystical Traveler Consciousness. An energy from the highest source of Light and Sound whose spiritual directive on Earth is awakening people to the awareness of the Soul. This consciousness always exists on the planet through a physical form.

Naccal Records. Spiritual records that precede the Akashic Records and which record all events from the beginning of time.

Negative Realms. *See Psychic, Material Realms.*

New Day Herald. MSIA's bimonthly newspaper.

90-Percent Level. That part of a person's existence beyond the physical level; that is, one's existence on the astral, causal, mental, etheric, and Soul realms.

Nof Ginosar. A hotel situated in an outstanding location, hugging the Sea of Galilee shores and nestling at the foot of Mount Arbel, facing the Golan-Heights. It is 10 kilometers north of Tiberius, and well-placed for all the main tourist attractions and sites in the Upper Galilee, Jordan Valley and Golan Heights. The hotel facilities include: air conditioned rooms, swimming pool, private beach, kosher restaurant, bar and cafeteria, seminar halls, and a souvenir shop.

NOW Productions. An operating group under the umbrella of MSIA, dedicated to recording, editing, and producing media from the seminars, speeches, workshops, and other public appearance events of John-Roger and John Morton.

Ocean of Love and Mercy. Another term for Spirit on the Soul level and above.

Ordination/Ordained. By an MSIA Minister and through the Melchizedek Priesthood is the process by which individuals are consecrated, that is set apart as clergy to perform various religious rites and ceremonies.

Outer Levels / Realms. The astral, causal, mental, etheric, and Soul realms above the Soul realm also exist outside a person's consciousness, but in a **greater way.** *See also Inner Levels/Realms.*

Peace Theological Seminary and College of Philosophy (PTS). A private, **nondenominational** institution presenting the spiritual teachings of MSIA.

Physical Realm. The earth. The psychic, material realm in which a being lives with a physical body.

Positive Realms. The Soul realm and the 27 levels above the Soul realm. *See also Psychic, Material Realms.*

Glossary

Preceptor Consciousness. A spiritual energy of the highest source, which exists outside creation. It has manifested on the planet in a physical embodiment once every 25,000 to 28,000 years.

Psychic Realms, Material Realms. The five lower, negative realms; namely, the physical, astral, causal, mental, and etheric realms. *See also Positive Realms.*

Queen Zenobia. (Approx. 240—after 274 A.D.) Zenobia was a Syrian woman who lived in the third century A.D. She was a Queen of the Palmyrene Empire and the second wife to king Septimius Odaenathus. Upon his death she became the ruler of the empire. In 269, she conquered Egypt, expelling the Roman prefect of Egypt, Tenagino Probus, whom she beheaded when he attempted a recapture. She then proclaimed herself Queen of Egypt also. She ruled until 274 A.D., when she was defeated and taken as hostage to Rome by the emperor Aurelian. Zenobia appeared in golden chains in Aurelian's military triumph parade in Rome. So impressed by her, Aurelian granted her clemency and freed Zenobia. Further, he granted her an elegant villa in Tibur (modern Tivoli, Italy). She lived in luxury and became a well-known philosopher, socialite, and Roman matron; prominent Romans are counted among her descendants.

Rukmini Canal. An opening in the void at the top of the etheric realm through which a person moves in consciousness into the Soul realm.

Sat Nam. The Lord of the Soul realm. Sat Nam ("True Name") is also the first individualized expression of the higher God.

SATs. *See Soul Awareness Tapes.*

S.E.'s. *See Spiritual Exercises.*

Seeding. A form of prayer to God for something that one wants to manifest in the world. It is done by placing a "seed" with (giving an amount of money to) the source of one's spiritual teachings.

Seminar. A talk given by John-Roger or John Morton, usually before a live audience; also, an audiotape or videotape of a talk either of them has given.

Soul. The extension of God individualized within each human being. The basic element of human existence, forever connected to God. The indwelling Christ, the God within.

Soul Awareness Discourses. A series of 144 booklets that students in MSIA read monthly as their spiritual study, for individual private and personal use only. They are an important part of the Traveler's teachings on the physical level.

Soul Awareness Tapes (SATs). Audiotapes of seminars given by John-Roger, for individual and private study only. Once a student has completed the 144 Soul Awareness Discourses, they subscribe to SATs. SATs are an important part of the Traveler's teachings on the physical level.

Soul Consciousness. A positive state of being. Once a person is established in Soul Consciousness, he or she need no longer be bound or influenced by the lower levels of Light.

Soul Realm. The realm above the etheric realm. The first of the positive realms and the true home of the Soul. The first level where the Soul is consciously aware of its true nature, its pure beingness, its oneness with God.

Glossary

Soul Transcendence. The process of moving the consciousness beyond the **psychic**, material realms and into the Soul realm and beyond.

Soul Travel. Traveling in Spirit to realms of consciousness other than the **physical realm**. Sometimes known as out-of-body experiences. This can be done in one's own inner realms, or in the outer realms, the higher spiritual realms. *See also Inner Levels/Realms and Outer Levels/Realms.*

Sound Current. The audible energy that flows from God through all realms. The spiritual energy on which a person returns to the heart of God.

Spirit. The essence of creation. Infinite and eternal.

Spiritual Exercises (S.E.'s). Chanting the Hu, the Ani-Hu, or one's **initiation tone**. An active technique of bypassing the mind and emotions by using a spiritual tone to connect to the Sound Current. Assists a person in breaking through the illusions of the lower levels and eventually moving into Soul consciousness. *See also Initiation Tone.*

Spiritual Eye. The area in the center of the head, back from the center of the forehead. Used to see inwardly. Also called the Third Eye.

Spiritual Hierarchy. The nonphysical spiritual forces that oversee this planet and the other psychic, material realms.

Ten-Percent Level. The physical level of existence, as contrasted with the 90 percent of a person's existence that is beyond the physical realm. *See also 90-Percent Level.*

Third Ear. The unseen spiritual ear by which we listen inwardly and hear the Sound Current of God.

Third Eye. *See Spiritual Eye.*

Tisra Til. The area in the center of the head, back from the forehead. It is here that the Soul energy has its seat and the Soul energy gathers.

Tithing. The Spiritual Practice of giving ten percent of one's increase to God and by giving it to the source of one's Spiritual Teachings.

Tone. The tone is an initiation sound that is the Name of God.

Traveler. A term/Slang used in MSIA for the Mystical Traveler or one that travels with Dr. John-Roger. *See Mystical Traveler.*

Traveler organizations. Dr. John-Roger has founded many organizations: Insight, MSIA, USM, Heartfelt, Scott J-R Productions, NOW, PTS, and many more.

Universal Mind. Located at the highest part of the etheric realm, at the division between the negative and positive realms. Gets its energy from the mental realm.

Wheel of 84. The reincarnation, re-embodiment cycle. *See also Karma and Reincarnation.*

*Those who sit very quietly in the silence
that roars the name of the Light and
do the most mundane jobs in love and devotion
are performing a beautiful service
that God sees as very great, indeed.*

– JOHN-ROGER, D.S.S.

Have the courage to follow your heart and intuition. They somehow already know what you truly want to become. Everything else is secondary.

– STEVE JOBS

APPENDIX III

References & Bibliography

ॷ

Garcia, Jesus. 1997 – 2008. *Unpublished Journals*.

Garcia, Jesus with John-Roger. 2008. *Spiritual Warriors*. DVD.

Hesse, Herman. 1956. *Journey to the East*. New York: Picador.

Holy Bible, New International Version. 1973, 1978, 1983. Grand Rapids, MI: The Zondervan Corporation. Book of Matthew, Chapter 18, Verse 20: "For where two or three come together in my name, there I am with them."

Source for Dr. John-Roger's *Spiritual Warrior: The Art of Living*, *The Way Out Book* quotes: www.lovingeachday.org

John-Roger. 1998. *Spiritual Warrior, The Art of Spiritual Living*. Los Angeles: Mandeville Press.

— 2007. *Fulfilling Your Spiritual Promise* (3 vols.). Los Angeles: Mandeville Press.

— 1989, 2000. *Loving Each Day*. Los Angeles: Mandeville Press.

— 1984. *Passage into Spirit*. Los Angeles: Baraka Books.

— 1986, 2000. *Relationships*. Los Angeles: Mandeville Press.

— 1973. *The Spiritual Promise*. Los Angeles: MSIA.

— 1980. 2004. *The Way Out Book*. Los Angeles: Mandeville Press.

— 2001. *The Wayshower*. Four CDs, No. 39011-CD. MSIA.

John-Roger with McWilliams, Peter. 1988. *You Can't Afford the Luxury of a Negative Thought*. Los Angeles: Prelude Press.

— 1990. *LIFE 101*. Los Angeles: Prelude Press.

— 1991. *DO IT! Let's Get Off Our Buts*. Los Angeles: Prelude Press.

— 1991. *Wealth 101*. Los Angeles: Prelude Press.

Kennedy, John F. 1955. *Profiles in Courage*. New York: Harper Collins Publishing.

Rolfe, Mona. 1976, 1992. *Initiation by the Nile*. London: C.W. Daniel Co., Ltd.

www.msia.org. Loving-Each-Day@msia.org

www.thedreamsofamaster.com

*There is a void in your soul, ready to be filled.
You feel it, don't you? You feel the separation
from the beloved. Invite Him to fill you up,
embrace the fire.*

– Rumi

The Kingdom of Heaven is within.

– JESUS THE CHRIST

About the Author

Jesus Garcia spent 26 years working for and learning from his spiritual teacher and Mystical Traveler, John-Roger, D.S.S. (known as "J-R"), founder of the Los Angeles-based Church of the Movement of Spiritual Inner Awareness (MSIA). Garcia was initiated into the Sound Current of God by John-Roger and ordained as a minister into the order of Melchizedek Priesthood by John Morton, who currently holds the keys to the Mystical Traveler Consciousness.

Garcia's first book, *The Love of a Master*—which detailed his nearly three decades as J-R's personal assistant, driver, and bodyguard—reached #1 Amazon Best-Selling status for the New Age Mysticism category in September 2017. In his second book, *The Dreams of a Master*, published in 2019, Garcia continues to take us on his journey of awakening after the passing of his beloved Traveler and friend, J-R, sharing his experiences and those of other initiates of even purer inner connection to Spirit and the Traveler than was ever realized on the physical level.

In creative collaboration, John-Roger and Garcia, a respected Hollywood cinema veteran, co-produced three feature movies: *Spiritual Warriors*, *The Wayshower*, and *Mystical Traveler*; and four short films, as "Scott J-R Productions." Since John-Roger's transition in 2014, Garcia has continued his ministry of sharing the spiritual teachings of J-R through movie screenings, Practical Spirituality workshops, and spiritual counseling to students and initiates of the Traveler all around the globe.

Previously, as a recognized actor, Garcia appeared on-screen in such popular films as *A Nightmare on Elm Street*, *Along Came Polly*, *We Were Soldiers*, *Spiritual Warriors*, *Collateral Damage*, and *Atlas Shrugged*. He currently resides in Santa Monica, California.

www.ingramcontent.com/pod-product-compliance
Lightning Source LLC
Chambersburg PA
CBHW031359040426
42444CB00005B/354